A treasure trove of prompts, provocations and practical exercises to help you spark new ideas, hone your craft and unleash your creativity.

In *A Year of Creative Thinking*, award-winning writer, director and film-maker Jessica Swale guides you through 366 fun and rewarding activities – one for every day of the year (including leap years!) – to fire up your imagination and flex your creative muscles.

You'll find a host of writing prompts and imaginative challenges to get you going, quick-fire exercises to help you focus on key aspects of craft (including inventing scenarios, writing dialogue, building subtext, creating atmosphere and plot, and developing your characters), and plenty of quirky and unusual challenges to test your limits and help you explore new avenues. Some are writing exercises, others encourage you to draw, to listen to music, to get outside and find inspiration in your surroundings. Work through the activities day by day, or dip in to suit your needs, the choice is yours!

Whether being creative is a professional goal, your aspiration or simply your hobby, you'll discover a storehouse of ideas and inspiration, along with insights from a wide range of literary and cultural figures – from T. S. Eliot to Quentin Tarantino, Jane Austen to Jimi Hendrix, Maya Angelou to George R. R. Martin, and Virginia Woolf to Paddington Bear.

Fun, engaging and pressure-free, this book is designed to supercharge your imagination and boost your creativity, helping you build a set of expressive tools that you can apply in all aspects of your life.

"Jessica Swale is one of the most inspiringly creative people I know, and in this book she's kind enough to share some of her spark and magic. It is a must-read for any creative spirit."
Zooey Deschanel

"Jessica has stitched together an endlessly inventive, engaging, accessible ejector-seat (parachute included) into the heart and soul of creativity itself. That energy flows through every page: challenging and guiding you into releasing your inner mad-genius. I wish there were more days in the year for more of her exercises!"
Inua Ellams

"The most brilliant book on creativity – so inspiring it will make you want to write your own book!"
Tom Fletcher

"An enticing treasure chest of inspiration for any writer or creative."
Deborah Frances-White

"This book will last you a lifetime, as you'll return again and again to these gems of wise, witty prompts and provocations – guaranteed to inspire not just your creativity, but your outlook on life in general."
Sabrina Mahfouz

"Charming, imaginative, practical and light-hearted, this is the perfect gift for anyone, young or not so young, wanting to kickstart their creativity and have fun while doing it."
Kate Mosse

"As I sit in my room smashing my head repeatedly against my laptop, it gives me (some) joy to report not all writers do the same. Jessica's book is a great big fantastic soulful fizzy key to make you think and work hopefully. 16th April is my favourite, but her point is: there are delights on every day of the year."
Jack Thorne

Jessica Swale

# A
# YEAR
## OF
# CREATIVE
# THINKING

*366 Daily Inspirations for Writers & Artists*

**N H B**

**NICK HERN BOOKS**
London
www.nickhernbooks.co.uk

# A Nick Hern Book

*A Year of Creative Thinking*
first published in Great Britain in 2025
by Nick Hern Books Limited,
The Glasshouse, 49a Goldhawk Road, London W12 8QP

Cover design by Heike Schüssler
Author photograph by Michael Wharley

Designed and typeset by Nick Hern Books, London
Printed and bound in the UK by Clays Ltd, Elcograf S.p.A.

A CIP catalogue record for this book
is available from the British Library

ISBN 978 1 83904 506 6

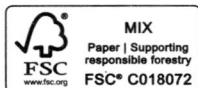

MIX
Paper | Supporting
responsible forestry
FSC
www.fsc.org FSC® C018072

www.nickhernbooks.co.uk/environmental-policy
Nick Hern Books' authorised representative in the EU is
Easy Access System Europe – Mustamäe tee 50, 10621 Tallinn, Estonia
*email* gpsr.requests@easproject.com

*For six women who have inspired me in my moments
of greatest silliness, solace, elation and imagination.*

*Gemma, Jen, Gugu, Claire, Harriet and Vicky.*

*You're the sisters I wish I'd had. My anam cara.*

# Contents

# Introduction

Hello. How lovely to meet you!

Thanks so much for coming, we're going to have a ball doing this creative thinking malarkey.

Don't worry if you're not sure about this. Maybe you bought this book in a fit of great energy and resolution, and now the idea of 'being creative' seems like massively hard work. You know what: it might be. But here in this book, you'll find an easy, pressure-free way to at least have a go. And even if you only do a little, I promise you it'll be worth it.

Putting time aside to be creative is *always* a good idea. To challenge your methods of thinking, give your hard-working, responsible brain a break from its usual tasks, to take time out of everyday life to explore a story, an idea, a picture or a song... it's fuel for the soul. The worst thing that's about to happen is that you create something that isn't genius. But who cares? You're creating! Practising. And practising makes... well, better. And it's a muscle, your creative imagination. It's like a puppy; it needs exercising or it'll develop bad habits, or get old and fat and never want to leave the house. No judgement on any readers who also might fit this description – age is wisdom and all bodies are beautiful, especially yours; today you look absolutely spiffing. I'm just saying, don't let that creative muscle get lazy, or it will seize up and give you grief and you'll never want to use it again.

So what is this book? Firstly, this book is pressure-free and non-judgemental. You are not required to do anything '*good*'. Exercise is exercise – you don't have to be an athlete. Doing any sort of exertion all adds to your fitness and stamina, and it's the same with creative activity. Stretching your imagination, challenging yourself to do some magical thinking, inventing, pondering, dreaming is *all* good for your brain. Scientifically, you are creating new neural pathways and strengthening cognitive functions. It's also very good for your mental health. Not to mention it's an excellent escape from the stresses of daily life. But most of all, it is *fun*. And we like fun. So enjoy this book and embrace the opportunities like a chance encounter with your favourite celebrity. Though in real life, maybe don't hug famous people – they might get upset and I wouldn't like to be responsible for that.

### How to Use This Book

You can use this book in any way you want. Although the book is arranged day by day, month by month, season by season, you can start wherever you like, whenever you like. And if you skip a day, or a month, or just roam around the book cherry-picking what you fancy, go for gold. It's your book and no one will ever know!

*Enjoy the kickabout, forget about the goals*

Let's be clear, the aim of this book isn't for you to complete an epic novel by the time you've finished it. The only goal is to find your most creative, most imaginative self, and to enjoy the act of invention as a means to expand your mind and happiness. You may have aspirations to be a writer by profession – or a creative artist, a lyricist, a musician, the next great sculptor of note… Or you may not. This might be a hobby. It might be a whim. Whatever brought you here, take the pressure off and enjoy the ride. The very least you'll do is have some ideas and stretch your brain. And who knows, maybe you *will* write an epic novel afterwards. But for now, just embrace the opportunity and use this book like a playground – try out all the slides and whizz down the imaginative zip wire. It'll be fun, I guarantee it.

*Building an arsenal of creative weapons*

Each of the exercises is designed to help you flex your creative muscles. Some are writing-focused, others tap into other forms of creative thinking, be it drawing, making, even walking and moving. And, once or twice, eating! By working holistically like this, challenging yourself in a multitude of different imaginative ways, you are building an arsenal of creative tools that you can then apply in all aspects of your life. If you do have a singular piece of work you are aiming to complete, you can use these exercises as a way to further explore and develop it, but that isn't the aim. By the time the year is out, if you follow these exercises you will have a whole plethora of new ideas to pick from, and I'll bet some of them will thrill you more than anything you've already started. So chill and take it slow, enjoy the daydreaming and imaginative thinking that the exercises encourage, and try to stay in the moment rather than looking for an end result.

*A question of form*

In order to build a diving board to leap off into your creative swimming pool, you have to choose a building material. And the easiest material to start with is a pen – and the art, writing. Whilst this book offers an array of different types of creative exercise, I focus on writing because through words you learn to create pictures, stories, people and tone. And words on a page can take you anywhere.

You may also have a form of writing you're most passionate about, be it poetry, prose or plays. This book offers you provocations in all of these. Most often you can choose which form to work in within each exercise. But if you do have a specific preference, try to challenge yourself to write in other forms too, as some of these exercises encourage. It is all building your personal skills bank, and nothing is wasted – often the best understanding of prose-writing comes after script work, as writing drama requires a dexterity with character and dialogue that will benefit any fiction you write afterwards.

The exercises in this book vary in scope, length, size and focus. You will encounter many varieties – some quick-fire, others long-form. Some are inspired by a writer whose birthday is celebrated on that particular day, encouraging you to use their techniques. Some are days of celebration or commemoration, from International Sweatpants Day to International Women's Day or Popcorn Day (yes, that's a thing). Some focus on the season, some on connecting with the wider world, looking for inspiration outside your writing space. Some are technical, investigating vocabulary, story, comedy, form, or breaking down structure to help you understand shape and story on a more molecular level. Some tap into memory. Some offer simple provocations. Some ask you to draw, to listen to music, to create something three-dimensional or just to spend some time thinking and observing.

I have purposefully mixed the exercises up so no two consecutive days are alike... which is why I recommend working through each day in order, if possible, so that you enjoy the variety as it is intended. You'll probably gravitate towards some exercises more than others, but do try everything, you may surprise yourself; often those that seem hardest initially will yield the greatest results.

My one piece of advice is this. Actually, *three*. Three pieces of advice, if I may:

1. Get yourself a notebook so you can keep all your writing together. Occasionally I may ask you to go back and revisit a piece you've written, so it's rather nice to have them in one place.

2. Get yourself a pen. Try doing these exercises by hand. Just try it. It's good for your brain, it's easier to avoid the distractions of that pesky internet, and it's good for your finger skills – so if you decide you hate writing, you can take up the guitar, get noodling and go join a rock band instead.

3. Start. Off you go! And enjoy!

# January

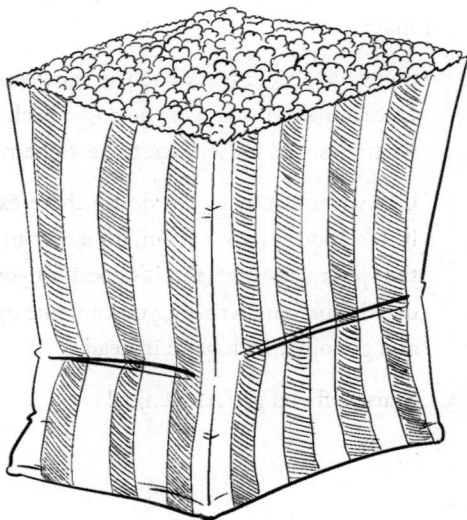

# 1st January

*"I am not at all in a humour for writing;
I must write on till I am."*
Jane Austen

Today is **International Commitment Day**. Sound fun? No, I don't think so either.

Commitment is a dirty word. Something about it is inherently off-putting. It's long. It's formal. You have to tense your mouth up to say it. It's the verbal equivalent of handcuffs. Welcome to 'International "You're Under Arrest" Day'. 'You Cannot Wriggle Out Of This Day.' '"I Thought This Was Going To Be Fun… Vegas Seemed Like Such A Good Idea… Who Knew It Was For Life?" Day.'

So why don't we rethink it and put it a different way? Let's make a pact. Never to think of writing as a commitment or chore. Make it a *choice*. And when you *choose* to do it, even if it's tough at the start, once you've got going, that's when you start to flow. And when you flow, that's when the fun starts. Do it once, you begin to *want* to do it again. And again. And the more you do it, the easier it gets – and the better your writing becomes. It's like a muscle. By the end of even the first week, those mini dumb-bells will be replaced by some super-strong sumo weights.

You've just got to get going. So let's begin! Like Austen said, even if you're not at all in a humour to write, do it for a bit, and you'll find the flow. Give yourself a break and let's start with an easy exercise…

Turn to the next blank page in your notebook and pick up your pen. You're going to write freehand for two sides. Don't censor yourself, don't edit. Write free-flow, which means try not to stop, and don't go back over it. Carry on until you've filled two pages and do it with no judgement. It is the verbal equivalent of turning the tap on. And your first line is this: 'I am a writer and, when I imagine myself writing, I…'

Try to put yourself into character. The character of a writer. A creative thinker. And imaginer. What does this look like? Who is this person – your creative self? Write about why you write. Who you might be. Go on a journey. Or rant about something. It's up to you. Just do it. And when you're done…

Congratulations! You've had a bout of creativity. You are now a writer. You have broken the seal. The journey has begun. If you want to read over, edit or rewrite, you can. But there's no need. The point is a writer is someone who puts words on the page – and that's you, my friend. Off we go.

# 2nd January

*"Far out in the uncharted backwaters of the unfashionable end of the western spiral arm of the Galaxy lies a small unregarded yellow sun."*
Douglas Adams, *The Hitchhiker's Guide to the Galaxy*

Space, time travel, black holes, AI... whether it's your genre or not, embrace the chance to dive into an alternate reality in this exercise on **Science Fiction Day**.

Choose one of the following prompts as a jumping-off point. Write for ten minutes. Don't overthink it, just start writing – and go with your gut. And if you're having a good time, carry on!

- Society is in a mess. Crime, depression, chaos, social media. Until the most unlikely unheroic person (a granny, a teenaged geek, a school cleaner) discovers that they actually have an extraordinary power and that they are... in fact... a superhero! And they're about to save a... What? That bit's up to you. Go wild! Let your imagination fly like a space cadet.

- On an otherwise unremarkable day, in an unremarkable kids' playground, in an unremarkable town, out of nowhere, a sinkhole appears, so deep no one can see the bottom. Then, a strange smell begins to emanate from it. Then odd noises. Someone has to volunteer to go and investigate...

# 3rd January

*"Not all those who wander are lost."*
J. R. R. Tolkein, *The Fellowship of the Ring*

I'm a restless writer. I don't like to sit in one place for too long, and I often have my best ideas when I'm wandering around. I like to walk in parks. Along rivers. Through little streets. Around markets. Where doesn't matter particularly. The important thing is that I am moving, and I am a giving my brain a chance to dream. To wander. No phone, no earphones, no podcasts, only my body – and my brain – wandering.

Today's exercise is to go for a wander. Simply walk and see where your imagination goes. No need to write anything down – unless you feel compelled to. Switch off the incoming technological buzz (that's non-negotiable), and just walk. Try not to *think* about anything specific.

Daydream. It's food for the writer's soul.

# 4th January

*"A reader lives a thousand lives before he dies...
The man who never reads lives only one."*
George R. R. Martin, *A Dance with Dragons*

Open a newspaper or magazine at random and look for a picture with lots of people in it. Pick someone who isn't the focus of the story. A random passer-by. Someone caught in the edge of the frame. Now write down the following 'facts' about them:

1. What is their name?

2. Their age?

3. Their occupation?

4. In one sentence, how would you describe them?

5. Where are they from?

6. What are they doing there?

7. Where were they going?

8. What happens in this moment? Or what is about to happen that changes their day – or their life – sending them off in a new direction?

For us to be interested in a character, the character has to *change* during the story. They have to be active: forced to do something, negotiate a situation, and therefore come out differently. Stories need drama – so work out what is happening or is about to happen to this person, and how it will change them, to ensure they're different *after* this photo, transformed by the day's event and how they dealt with it. And then write their story.

# 5th January

Creative storytelling often comes from the way we join disparate ideas in new and surprising ways: the pin-to-pin threads on a police suspect board, the unusual links between familiar things... the embracing and intertwining of random ideas.

Today you're going to write something using the following four elements. Unrelated... until now!

- A scarlet hat.

- A tourist information centre on the slopes of a mountain.

- A ukulele.

- A woman with an irregular heartbeat.

JANUARY

8

# 6th January

*"Be less curious about people
and more curious about ideas."*
Marie Curie

Today is the day of **Epiphany**. You don't have to be a Christian to like this celebration. I'm not, I just like the word. *Epiphany!* It sounds exciting. Pop-py. Like – *zing!* An idea has landed, and it's fantastic!

Epiphanies don't come easily. And don't panic, today's task isn't to have one. Instead, it's an exercise inspired by Marie Curie and her notion that inspiration often arises from finding things out. And look at what she did with her life. I bet the day of her epiphany was a good one. 'Zing! Radium! Now there's an idea.'

So today, you're not going to write, you're going to read. Pick a book, article or newspaper that you wouldn't normally read (tabloid newspapers excluded; read something good). It doesn't have to be *hard*, but the content should be outside your go-to topics of interest. For me, that would mean an article about business or finance. Or football. Or a book about hedge-trimming.

Have a read, and see where it takes you. And if you feel inspired, write a little – a paragraph or two – about a person in the world that you're reading about. Perhaps my next character will be a hedge-trimmer. Who knows? Certainly once I've read that book, I'll be able to write that character with much more nuance than I could yesterday.

# 7th January

*"I like good, strong words that mean something."*
Louisa May Alcott, *Little Women*

Today we're a week into the new year, and I don't know about you, but this tends to be when all my good new resolutions fail. Whoever thought giving up alcohol in the coldest, quietest, post-celebratory slump of a month was a good idea? And if you live anywhere near me, it's usually rainy. Plus, my Christmas chocolate has just about run out. It's a sad day.

Until *now*! Because today's exercise is a joy-bringer. Write down all your favourite words. That's it. Stick the heating on, put your feet up and write them down. Long ones, short ones, funny ones; they can be names and place names as well as 'proper' words.

I like words that are fun to say. I also like words that sound like music. I'll give you a few of mine to jump-start the proverbial car: Mellifluous. Fandango. Fling. Sot. Clodpoll. Bollocks. Atoll. Mum. Hodgelet. Startle. Snack.

# 8th January

*"Let's be reasonable and add an eighth day to the week that is devoted exclusively to reading."*
Lena Dunham

Lena Dunham knows what she's talking about. She's a fantastic screenwriter – and that's partly because she is a devourer of the written (and filmed) word. Reading expands your ideas, references, vocabulary and worldview.

Today, pick four books from your shelves that you haven't read. Get a cuppa, raid the biscuit tin, get comfortable and just read. Read the first chapter of all four books. But do it with a writer's eye. Try to observe what the writer is doing. How they draw you in. How they share their prose, their choice of vocabulary, use of dialogue, character. What works for you? What doesn't? Which of the four is the book you want to carry on reading?

You don't need to write anything down; just park all these ideas in your brain-bank and remember them for the next time you're writing.

# 9th January

*"The first writing of the human being was drawing,
not writing."*
Marjane Satrapi

It's time for an art task! Today you're going to create a comic strip or storyboard. It's quite a skill to tell a story in a number of images… it's a great exercise in how to be succinct.

Take a story you know well. It could be a favourite fairytale, a short story, a myth, or you could choose a section from a novel. And storyboard it as follows: write down the main points of the story. Try to reduce these to eight bite-sized pieces. Work out what the image would be that encapsulates that. And remember that storyboards require action to make the images sing. Set-dressing does not a good comic strip make.

Now draw it! When you've done it, have a think about how you have managed to tell your story with an incredibly minimal number of words. What from the original story was dispensable? What was essential? Put this in your writing brain for later when you're editing your own work.

# 10th January

Today let's focus on creating atmosphere.

Writers use many techniques to do this. Sometimes writing sensorially, using all five senses. Sometimes writing sparsely – to keep us on our toes and on the edge of our seats. They might use pace to create tension. Use heat, light, a sense of movement to create a landscape that allows the reader to find themselves there. Or drip-feed us information to build the drama.

Look at how Jeanine Cummins hooks us into her nail-biting thriller *American Dirt*. It's the story of mother and son on the run across South America, trying to escape the cartel. It's not my usual fare, but from page one it was so visually arresting in her use of description, that I found I couldn't put it down. It opens:

> *'One of the very first bullets come in through the open window above the toilet where Luca is standing. He doesn't immediately understand that it's a bullet at all, and it's only luck that it doesn't strike him between the eyes. Luca hardly registers the mild noise it makes as it flies past and lodges into the tiled wall behind him. But the wash of bullets that follows is loud, booming, and thudding,* clack-clacking *with helicopter speed. There is a raft of screams, too, but that noise is short-lived, soon exterminated by the gunfire. Before Luca can zip his pants, lower the lid, climb up to look out, before he has time to verify the source of that terrible clamour, the bathroom door swings open and Mami is there.'*

Immediately, there's drama, character and *specific* peril, as it becomes obvious that Luca is a child. That's what hooked me. Peril of an innocent – and so vividly realised. We know we're in for a roller-coaster ride.

Now choose a tense scenario – something with high stakes. Go on, make your characters' lives as difficult a possible! Three people stuck in an underwater cave as water is rising. A tourist, lost on a jungle trek, who thinks they have refound their group… only to discover it's a pack of dangerous animals. Or a nervy dad in a queue for a bungee jump… with a crazed bungee instructor strapping him in. Have a go. Just a paragraph. See what drama you can create in only a few words.

# 11th January

*"To survive, you must tell stories."*
Umberto Eco

Imagine that it's the end of the world. Everyone has been extinguished... everyone but the residents of one place. Everyone there is (so far) blissfully unaware that the rest of the world is no longer. They are the only survivors, and between them, will have to build their own society. When they find out, of course.

Who are they? Oh, so many options. There's obviously a huge, serious tale to tell here – if you choose a nuclear submarine or a government bunker. But what other choices are there? Many are *way* more fun, especially if you want to write something comedic. What happens if the last people on earth are the contestants of an annual morris-dancing convention in the village hall? Or a coachful of retired singletons with romantic aspirations, on a package tour of Peru? Or a family that cannot stand the sight of each other?

And what the hell has happened to the rest of the world? Let your imagination run wild and see what you come up with. You can write your scenario or draw it in a series of vignettes.

# 12th January

*"I like books that aren't just lovely but have memories in themselves. Just like playing a song, picking up a book again, the memories can take you back to another place or another time."*
Emma Watson

Today is **National Youth Day**. What's your most vivid childhood memory?

Write it… twice.

Once in the first person ('I…'), honestly, as close to reality as you can remember.

Then a second time, now in the third person ('he/she/they/Ali/the man…'), viewing yourself as a character. In this second version, feel free to play around with the truth, rewriting it to be a story based on a memory – allowing yourself poetic licence.

# 13th January

*"A wise bear always keeps a marmalade sandwich
in his hat in case of emergency."*
Paddington Bear

So often it's the esoteric details of a character that make them memorable. A habit, a tic, a distinctive style. Or, in Paddington's case, his preference of sandwich filling.

For today's exercise (on the birthday of Paddington's creator, **Michael Bond**), go to your fridge or kitchen cupboard, and choose an item of food. Bring it back to your desk and have a look at it. Who (other than you) might eat this?

Write down four options for a person who might love – or hate – this food. I want you to choose four so that you go beyond the most clichéd choice. A pepperoni sausage, for example, would be an obvious pick for an Italian gangster or an overweight telly addict. But wouldn't you rather read about the high-profile vegan campaigner, who cannot help her secret addiction, knowing that her reputation will be destroyed if anyone finds out?

Now write a paragraph or two in which your character has a confrontation with the food. Perhaps they come home late at night after the most dramatic day of their life and this brings them comfort. What happened that day? Or have they secreted it on their person because they're about to face – what? – and they can't do without it?

One tip. I would strongly suggest you sample this food, so that you can write about it with more sensory detail. I hope you picked something delicious and not a bottle of hot sauce.

# 14th January

*"Organising is what you do before you do something,
so that when you do it, it is not all mixed up."*
A. A. Milne

Today, on **Organise Your Home Day**, you're going to organise your writing space.

Just like a dish that tastes extra delicious because it's beautifully presented, take your environment seriously. Make a space for yourself in which you will enjoy writing.

Consider the following: Is it light enough? Is it tidy? Does it smell nice? Would you burn a candle while you write? Listen to music? Do you want to be able to see outside? Or be free of distractions? Will you write better staring at a blank wall, or a wall covered in pictures and quotes that inspire you? Would a pot plant or flowers make you feel full of the joys of spring... or aggravate your hay fever?

Or, if you are writing in public – in a library or a café perhaps – think about finding the best environment *within* this space. Perhaps you always sit at the big, crowded tables in the library, but have you explored all the floors? Maybe there's a nook. A book nook. Maybe there's a quiet corner that catches the sunlight. What kind of books might inspire your ideas? You don't have to sit in fiction. Maybe you want to be steeped in history. Or trains. Or cookery books.

And if you're in a café, where are you sitting? Some people love to write in a noisy space as it can, conversely, help you concentrate. Does the smell of coffee pick you up or distract you with its temptations? Might you be better going to the park and sitting on a bench? Even if you think you have no options – question that. Perhaps you do.

This is your chance make yourself a treat of a writer's space. Even if you don't have a designated nook, wherever you write, try to make it as personal and inspiring as possible.

JANUARY

# 15th January

*"I know it is wet and the sun is not sunny,*
*but we can have lots of good fun that is funny."*
Dr. Seuss's *The Cat in the Hat*

It's **National Hat Day,** but let's *not* write a story about hats.

Today's exercise turns to the well-known genius Theodor Seuss Geisel, better known as Dr. Seuss. Author of lots of weird and fantastical children's books, he was a thinker, an educator and a rather eccentric guy who regularly challenged himself to write with restrictions. His most famous book, *The Cat in the Hat* (tenuous 'Hat Day link' here), remarkably uses only 255 words.

No one thought that something so simple and, frankly, odd would ever work, let alone be a hit. But when the copies began flying off the shelves, Dr. Seuss and his editor knew they were on to something. His editor then bet him that he couldn't write anything again with such a limited vocabulary pool. Of course, Dr. Seuss saw this as a challenge and a short time later came back with *Green Eggs and Ham*. And how many different words are in the story? Fifty. That's it. No wonder it's such an odd book! And yet it's a bestseller multiple times over.

So here's your challenge. You're going to try to write a story using a vocabulary of only fifty words. It needs to rhyme. So I begin by finding two or three pairs of words that give you some characters and sense of tone. This will probably take up ten words. For example:

PET, MET

FROG, DOG

HORSE, COURSE

MAN, PLAN

WEED, DEED

SNOG, BOG

FREE, ME

BEE, TREE

Even from these simple pairs you could think up any number of very short tales. Pick a couple of pairs of words to give you a starting point, then start building. A warning: by the time you start adding linking words your fifty-word limit gets gobbled up very quickly, so don't plan too much, just get going! I'd heartily recommend reading *Green Eggs and Ham* before you do.

And when you're done, do yourself a favour and get yourself a copy of my favourite of all his books, *Oh, the Places You'll Go!* It's inspiration for life – and it's wonderful.

And if you *still* want to write a story about hats, then here goes. As a second exercise, write your version of the beloved *Mr Benn* books. For those who don't remember them, Mr Benn would visit a fancy-dress shop, choose a costume, then find himself stepping out of the shop in the world of that adventure (picking a suit of armour, he'd walk out into Camelot, for example). So write a Mr Benn story – but with a hat! And then feel very smug that you did two tasks today. Pat on the back for you. Perhaps purchase yourself a lovely hat as a reward.

# 16th January

*"I haven't been everywhere, but it's on my list."*
Susan Sontag

If you could arrive anywhere – *anywhere* – at any time in history, where would it be?

On **Susan Sontag's birthday,** and inspired by her quote above, for today's exercise, create a scenario in which your character (it could be you or someone else) opens a door and finds themselves in a completely different time and place. Build the world they encounter as fully as possible. Why are they there? What happens next?

Do this either in words or pictures, whichever gives you the bigger thrill today.

# 17th January

*"I love the silent hour of night,*
*For blissful dreams may then arise,*
*Revealing to my charmed sight*
*What may not bless my waking eyes!"*
Anne Brontë, 'Night'

Happy birthday, **Anne Brontë**! In the spirit of her poem, today's exercise is really simple.

Choose three people. One of them is you, the other two are characters you can make up. Perhaps based on people you've observed: someone in the supermarket, someone on the bus, or… invent someone. Make sure the other two people are quite different from you, in lifestyle, in terms of their role in society, age, and so on.

For each of these three people, think about what they dream about. What would make their lives better? What would bring them happiness – not just material wealth – real happiness? Jot down a list for each, but don't rush. Allow yourself time to be inventive. Perhaps your supermarket-checkout teenager has recently lost a parent, which would explain why they're always cross when they serve you. Perhaps the 1920s flapper that you invented has dreams of leaving her frustrating family behind, and running away to pursue the high life in New York. And you? What do you really want? Think carefully. It takes time to dig deep.

When you've made your three lists, choose the character whose dream is the most interesting to write about. Now, observing the character from the outside, write a short piece in which the character expresses their dream. It could be simply in their heads: 'She flopped down on the dune and closed her eyes…' Or perhaps they're in conversation with someone else. Up to you. Dream big and have fun.

# 18th January

*"Vocabularies are crossing circles and loops. We are defined by the lines we choose to cross or to be confined by."*
A. S. Byatt

Words, words, words! As Hamlet says. Today, seeing as it's **National Thesaurus Day**, let's play with them.

Find a paragraph in a book or magazine, the plainer the writing style, the better. And now rewrite it using a thesaurus.

Discover a melange of lyrical lexicon inscribed deftly within a conglomeration of verbal effluence, within a writerly folio or perchance an unsophisticated publication – the more abundantly boundless in verbal dexterity, the most wondrously superior – and grasp this singular opportunity to use your erudition to refashion the base, ignoble verbiage into an explosive kaleidoscope of ingenious utterances.

Use the most florid, most imaginative, most descriptive language you can. Just as I did.

Have fun with it. I give you full permission to be as over-the-top as you like… enjoy the vast wealth of language at your disposal.

# 19th January

*"When people ask me if I went to film school I tell them no, I went to films."*
Quentin Tarantino

Today is **National Popcorn Day**. Hoorah! To celebrate, you have two tasks.

One: get yourself a big ole bag of the stuff, sit down and have a munch. Or even better, pop it yourself on the hob – there's little in life more satisfying than the popping explosions of corn pinging against the pan lid.

Now, once you're settled with snack in hand, let that scent send you right back to your favourite times in the movies. List a few of your favourite films. And then ponder on this: Nearly every film follows the same basic structure. A *character* exists in the status quo, until they encounter a *problem*. They must then *tackle* that problem/adversary/ obstacle, in order to overcome it. It's so simple, but you'll find it's true of nearly every movie. Essentially, structure runs like this:

1. *Set-up*: Here's our character getting on with their life…

2. *Inciting Incident*: …Until X happens/arrives/changes to challenge that. *Problem!*

3. *Journey and Progress*: In which our protagonist has to tackle the problem, win the girl, solve the puzzle, save the earth, usually by initially making progress, before…

4. *The Turning Point* (*midpoint and dramatic build*): When things get much worse. These stages (numbers 3, 4 and 5) are the central arc, the adventure, some wins, some losses, ramping towards a middle when – uh-oh – major setback! Things get worse and worse; in fact, can they get any worse? Now we're on a roller coaster and it turns out: Yes! They can get worse – they

can reach the peak of all disaster. There seems to be no coming back. The lovers hate each other. The world is about to be annihilated. The time is about to run out... until...

5.  *Climax/Resolution*: The story climaxes and resolves. Usually with our heroes winning, although the resolution doesn't have to be good. In Hollywood, of course, it usually is: the aliens are defeated, the gal gets her guy, the planet is saved from apes/zombies/massive chunks of space junk.

Have a think about your favourite movies and see if you can analyse them within this five-act structure. And remember: they don't have to be literal. Whilst adventure films like *Back to the Future* or *The Goonies* obviously follow the structure of adventure, most films share this shape when you really look at it, regardless of genre. Think of the adventure as the character's internal journey.

Now, have a go at it yourself. Choose a simple premise. Think of a hero, give them a 'normal life', and then consider what bombshell might drop on them to send them off on an adventure. A simple way to do it is to think of a person who has a very specific comfort zone, then put them in a scenario where they have to confront it. The man who has terrible vertigo, whose children get stranded on top of a mountain and will only survive if he can get them down. The woman who has become a house-bound recluse since her husband died, who is offered the chance of a lifetime... which requires an international trip. The kid who is determined to be a Premier League footballer... but lives in the Arctic.

Then follow the five-point plan to write the broadest of outlines for your film.

There you go, Tarantino-in-the-making! Hopefully with a bit less blood and gore. And if you'd rather draw your five points as a storyboard, feel free. Get creative.

When you're done, hold on to this, we're going to come back to it tomorrow. And if you weren't intending to write tomorrow, too late! You've already begun, so now you have no excuse. I'll see you then.

25

# 20th January

*"Cinema is a matter of what's in the frame and what's out."*
Martin Scorsese

Today is an unusual day in this book because it's Part Two of an exercise. Ooh, a doubler! So if you didn't do yesterday's exercise, I'd recommend going back and doing that first.

But if you did: have a house point/gold star/champion's cup, you swot. You should be wielding your five-point film plan, all ready to shoot your Oscar-worthy epic. Or at least, you have a rough outline of a story that's fit for purpose. That's cool too. We can't all be Scorsese.

So you have your five story points. Now here's the magic. Each of these 'story beats' will be quite unwieldy. For each one, you are going to divide it into three parts – a beginning, middle and ending – giving you mini-structures within your super-structure. Let's look at Beat 1 – the set-up – as an example:

Here's our character getting on with their life. You know that in the next beat there will be an inciting incident that turns their world upside down. So in your set-up you need to… guess what… set that up! You can use your set-up to make the inciting incident as powerful as possible, by working out what would destabilise your protagonist the most.

Use the three points of your mini-structure well. Make them into a story – and ensure your character/s are in a different position at the end of this beat, to the beginning. So in the set-up:

- *Beginning*: Establish your character – where, when, who, their situation.

- *Middle*: What's happening to that character, what's the mini-drama of the present – they are likely to be doing something or trying to.

- *Ending*: Now, ramp up to set up your inciting incident – the climax of this first beat.

By way of example, let's use the classic story of Charles Dickens's *A Christmas Carol*. Read the short story, or watch one of the many film adaptations.

In the set-up, Dickens establishes the world, who Scrooge is, and works up towards the inciting incident – the moment when Scrooge meets the three ghosts, and when he begins his journey into the past, present and future. He needs to reach that point during the set-up, which works as follows:

- *Beginning of the set-up*: Scrooge is an old miser who despises Christmas and is mean to everybody. No one believes he will ever change. He is stuck in his ways and determined not to celebrate Christmas, nor allow anyone working for him to do so either.

- *Middle of the set-up*: This part *advances* that plot, making Scrooge even more mean and sending a ripple of 'something's gonna happen'. He refuses an invitation to join his nephew's family for Christmas, as he doesn't see why anyone would celebrate Christmas. He allows poor Bob Cratchit, who works for him, one day off, but that's all.

- *End of the set-up*: This section moves towards the climax of your 'set-up' beat, teeing up the big change. A ghost appears with a warning for Scrooge. It's Marley – his very old and very dead business partner – who tells Scrooge that he must change his ways before it's too late, and that three more ghosts will vist him to make sure he does. Duh-duh-duh! That's the set-up; time to move on to the second beat...

You should spend some time breaking down each of your five beats into three-part structures, and then you'll have fifteen beats in your story, giving you your route-markers as you write it. Congratulations!

Now, as a bonus exercise that I would heartily recommend, in celebrating **National Camcorder Day** (who knew?!), try coming up with an image for each of them. You can either:

- Draw them.

- Take photographs, or...

- (and this is where you win *all* the points) Record some short video clips.

If you choose the last option (and you can use a smartphone rather than a camcorder, of course): Ta-dah! You already have a movie. It's short, fine – but it's a full fifteen story beats, which, let's face it, is an awful lot more storytelling than some of the movies out there.

# 21st January

*"The very reason I write is so that I might not sleepwalk through my entire life."*
Zadie Smith

Today your task is to get outside and do some exercise.

Don't look at me like that. It *is* **International Sweatpants Day**, and whilst you might hope that that would mean your task is to sit on your sweet ass and do jack-all, it ain't.

Here's the thing: exercise gives you endorphins, sends blood to your brain and gets it firing on all cylinders... and that is great news for your imagination. It's science. Believe me.

There's a vast amount of evidence that people have their best ideas when they're out moving their bodies. Check out Haruki Murakami's *What I Talk About When I Talk About Running*. He is an astonishing writer who regards his daily exercise routines as a key part of his creative process. And though, unlike Murakami, I am no marathon runner, I either walk or run every day before I begin work, regardless of the weather. It clears my head and gets me in a creative space to start writing.

So, whether you want to walk or run, that's up to you, but your task today is to take yourself outside and move quickly. And crucially DON'T LISTEN TO ANYTHING!

I know, you're probably used to stepping out with your earphones on, constantly feeding your brain with *stuff*. But if you want to get to the deeper parts of your imagination, the cerebral bit, the subconscious, then you have to allow yourself to daydream. And daydreaming only happens when you go through a boredom threshold.

Most of the time our brains are overstimulated. They're used to a constant barrage of information. You are always feeding your brain with sound, thoughts, to-do lists, feedback, podcasts, gossip, worries and plans. And when you go out and don't listen to something, that quiet can make you panic. Quick! Put something in my ears! I can't possibly listen to my own thoughts!

Get over it. Previous generations used to walk for miles without earphones and (except for plague, rampant misogyny, leeches and the constant threat of bandits) they were perfectly content to listen to their own thoughts.

So take your earphones out. You will then inevitably go through what I like to technically term the 'chatter' phase, which is a mixture of your brain shouting 'give me something to listen to' and you making mental to-do lists. Only once you've had all those conscious thoughts and ignored them, will you transition into the next phase… the 'bored now, I'll just swim around in the subconscious' dreamy phase. And that is the magic bit.

This subconscious deep-dive is where you have ideas. You probably won't even know it, but magically, that idea that you've been toying with might – when you revisit it – somehow have been expanded. And when you run, or walk, and your brain has a wonderful 'rush of blood to the head', you're helping this creative process no end.

So today I don't want you to write anything. Just get out and get the juices flowing, enjoy your subconscious wanderings and know that you're giving yourself a great gift – and when you write tomorrow it will inevitably be a work of genius.

# 22nd January

*"We write to taste life twice,*
*in the moment and in retrospect."*
Anaïs Nin

Here's what we do today… we are going to celebrate the many excellent things in life. It's **Celebration of Life Day**. So think of the things that make you happy. Treat yourself. And enjoy every moment of the experience. And write nothing down. Go on, I give you permission.

Maybe a treat for you is a walk in a forest. Or a really good cup of coffee. Or a massage. Or a stroll with a mate. Or fifteen minutes on your own without the family banging on the door. Each to his own. Mine is a cinnamon swirl from a Danish bakery. If you live near one, try it. Those buns are *something else*.

When you've organised your treat, you're sitting with your bun/coffee/crisp, cold pint in a pub garden, I want you to take this little bit of time to really *enjoy* the experience. Feel it. Savour it. Walk, drink or eat meditatively. Think about how it feels. The detail. The flavours. The spice-bazaar scent of the cinnamon; the pillow-puff texture of the sweet bread; the childhood-birthday taste of the icing; the delight of eating something *purely* for pleasure, in the full glorious knowledge that it has absolutely no nutritional value. Yum.

And that's it. As writers we need to feed off our experiences, notice the world around us in order to write with nuance, with a sense of individuality, with honesty. And God knows there's often enough suffering or difficulty to draw on for the dark moments in our writing. So today, give yourself some self-care, some you-time, and maybe one day it'll be useful material for a bit of writing. And if it isn't – who cares? It was a lovely cinnamon swirl.

# 23rd January

*"I prefer the pen. There is something elemental about the glide and flow of nib and ink on paper."*
James Robertson, *The Testament of Gideon Mack*

Today, it's **National Handwriting Day**. So even if you usually write on a laptop, you're going to write on paper. Put aside the technology, we're going back to basics, and it's wonderful. Writing by hand often helps you think differently, I find.

Find a comfortable spot and get ready. You are going to write an internal monologue for a character who has an important letter to write. You're not writing the letter; you're writing the character's thoughts as they're prepping to write the letter. Their motivation. Their worries. Their talking themselves into it... or out of it? Who are they, how do they speak and why exactly is this letter they are planning to write *so* important?

Go for high stakes. Make this a life-changing letter. Your protagonist might be imparting a secret. Are they pregnant... by another man? Are they telling their son that he is actually adopted? Or (in a different genre) that they are not of the same planet? Or are they finally admitting that they are guilty of the crime that ruined the recipient's life? Give your character some emotions to chew on.

# 24th January

*"We look before and after,*
*And pine for what is not:*
*Our sincerest laughter*
*With some pain is fraught;*
*Our sweetest songs are those that tell*
*  of saddest thought."*
Percy Bysshe Shelley, 'To a Skylark'

Today, it's **National Compliment Day**! And boy, do you look swell!

Make sure you say something nice to someone – and to yourself. Which brings me to your task. We're writing dialogue. For two characters. And it's all about subtext.

The task is inspired by Oscar Wilde's famous tea-drinking scene in Act Two, Scene Two of *The Importance of Being Earnest*, when Cecily and Gwendolen make 'polite conversation', but in every line purposefully insult each other in a battle of wits. It's brilliant. If you don't know it, read it before you begin.

You are going to invent two very polite characters who hate each other. Who are they and what is their vendetta? Their aim within the dialogue is to utterly undermine and traduce the other, thereby winning the proverbial points. But the politer they are, the better.

Choose a formal or polite scenario – that's why the tea-drinking is ideal. Where are your two characters that they have to be utterly *lovely* to each other, and yet not mean a word?

# 25th January

*"A woman must have money and a room of her own
if she is to write fiction."*
Virginia Woolf, A Room of One's Own

Today it's **Virginia Woolf's birthday** *and,* in her honour, 'A Room of One's Own' Day... apparently. So let's turn to her for a tip to kick-start today's task. She advised writers that 'any captivating protagonist should be someone you can imagine in "the centre of all sorts of scenes".'

You're going to create a character piece in three parts, each set in a different location. Firstly, choose your protagonist, someone whom we associate with a specific place. An ER doctor, for example, or the owner of a stately home, or a zookeeper. Your first scene is going to be set in their natural territory, seeing them do what we would expect them to do. Write this as a paragraph or draw it – up to you.

Now we are going to twist it. Your second scene is going to be set somewhere we would never expect to find that person. Put your champion boxer in a crochet club in a church hall. Enjoy exploring how and why they are there – and what new light it sheds on them.

Your third scene can be set anywhere you choose, though it must be a new location. The aim is to complete and resolve the story. Pull the threads of Scenes One and Two together. Woolf encouraged writers to create characters full of contradictions: the timid must have a tenacious streak, the most interesting tough guys might have a love of something sweet-smelling or beautiful.

By putting your familiar characters in wildly contrasting settings, that's when they start to become complex... and therefore more real. We are all a mass of contradictions, as someone said once.

# 26th January

"A DEFINITION NOT FOUND
IN THE DICTIONARY
Not leaving: an act of trust and love,
often deciphered by children."
Markus Zusak, *The Book Thief*

Happy **Australia Day**! There are many great exports from Down Under, but one of my favourites is Markus Zusak's gorgeous book, *The Book Thief*. It's about a young girl in Second World War Germany who, amidst many other adventures, discovers her love of reading and ends up trying to save books that the Nazis have banned. It's a great read.

Today's exercise is about saving stories. I wouldn't usually advocate attempting to rewrite someone else's narrative. But here's the exercise:

Think of a favourite book of yours. Imagine it's been banned, and the only way of preserving it is to attempt to and write it for posterity. You are going to write the first page or so, without looking at the original. You probably have no memory of how it starts – but remember the exercise… the book has been banned, you have no access to it, so whatever's important about it – the character, the location, the set-up – try to recreate it as best you can.

Many good books have fantastic openings that stick in your mind… Who can forget the pea scene from *Captain Corelli's Mandolin* or the description of the heat-charred landscape in *The Grapes of Wrath*? So, a word of warning: this exercise is hard! Even if you remember an opening scene well, you're likely to find recreating this detail for yourself a challenge. But embrace it. And consider what was important to *you*. What struck *you*. And when you don't remember, fill in the blanks. Imagine you are sending your opening paragraphs to a publisher and you need to convince them how delicious and wonderful this book is. It won't survive without you!

Think how the original writer wrote, as far as you remember. Which person is it written in? Does the writer write simply or in long, florid sentences? Do they tend to jump straight into action or is their writing descriptive? What perspective is it written from?

Then, when you're done, go back to the original book. This is the point at which you gape and marvel at how brilliantly that original writer wrote page one, and how you remembered nothing correctly, and how yours may pale in comparison. If this is the case: *don't worry*, that's what you're supposed to think! That writer spent months, years most likely, writing and rewriting this. And they originated it so it has the added magic of being written from the heart.

Notice what choices that writer made. How did they set up the story? It must have hooked you when you read it; how did they achieve that? It's a really useful exercise to look at their work having tried to emulate it yourself.

If you have the time (and you're not wallowing in existential despair at this point), you can move on to part two of this exercise. You've looked at the writer's way. Now put it to one side, consider what you've just learnt about why their writing is so effective, and have another go. See how your writing changes. Jot down what you've learnt. Then put your feet up and read the rest of their novel again – there's nothing more delightful than returning to a brilliant book.

# 27th January

*"Our battered suitcases were piled on the sidewalk again; we had longer ways to go. But no matter, the road is life."*
Jack Kerouac, *On the Road*

Today it's **National Geographic Day** and your task is to imagine you are a scriptwriter for a natural history programme. Think David Attenborough, *Blue Planet*, *The Call of the Wild*...!

Pick an obscure place in the world – a natural landscape where you find interesting animals. Now spend ten minutes googling the wildlife of that location and pick an animal that you are going to feature.

Write your narration, finding a way to interest the audience in this fascinating and surprising species. What habits do they have? What do they eat? How do they mate? What makes them quirky? What will draw your audience in? Seek out a tone for your presenter to create an easy relationship with their audience. The right balance of science and fact with intriguing detail and anthropomorphic observations (where animals take on human characteristics) is often the magic formula.

# 28th January

*"I declare after all there is no enjoyment like reading!
How much sooner one tires of anything than of a book! –
When I have a house of my own, I shall be miserable if I have
not an excellent library."*
Jane Austen, *Pride and Prejudice*

Today is a writing-prompt day, inspired by the wonder that is Jane Austen's *Pride and Prejudice*, first published on this day in 1813.

In the book, Elizabeth Bennet and Mr Darcy both have moments of thinking back to their past actions and attitudes towards each other, and cursing themselves for their pride – or prejudice. Your task today is to write a monologue, in your own voice, about a memory that fills you with embarrassment.

If you like, as an antidote afterwards, rewrite it – and in doing so rewrite history to give it a different outcome. Catharsis.

# 29th January

*"You must stay drunk on writing
so reality cannot destroy you."*
Ray Bradbury

Okay, okay, bear with me. I'm going to suggest you take Bradbury's advice quite literally. If you have no reason not to (if you have or ever have had any issues with alcohol, then genuinely, please avoid) – in the interest of experimenting – try writing today after a couple of drinks. Choose something you're working on, or write a poem. If you have no 'go-to' project, then have a go at writing what happens next based on one of these four opening-line options:

- If we had seen the sign, everything would have been different.
- It was the way she pushed her hair behind her ear that first caught my attention.
- Crack. Crack. Crack.
- I always knew that I would die on the first of May.

But write it a bit tipsy. Have a glass of wine and then write. You may be amazed how much a slight hazy and a carefree (or careless?!) approach allows you to write with less self-censorship. It can often be useful to stop thinking too much and just write. Let your subconscious do the work, see what it regurgitates (okay, don't drink *that* much)…

I'm not going to tell you that some of my best pieces of work originated after rather an indulgent night out, but just occasionally… Just try it.

However, if you don't drink, instead put on a swinging song and dance with all your energy for the whole track. Get out of breath. Lose yourself in the music, then sit down immediately and write uncensored. The fact your body is distracted by music and catching your breath will help you write spontaneously without overthinking.

# 30th January

*"You can always edit a bad page. You can't edit a blank page."*
Jodi Picoult

Let's practise editing, but without the pressure of working on something precious yet. It's just an exercise. You are going to set your timer and free-write for five minutes, non-stop, on one of the following three subjects:

• Claustrophobia.

• School gym kit.

• A memory of a colour.

Write from a character's perspective – your own is fine, or pick a relevant character for your tale. After five minutes, stop wherever you got to.

Now, set the timer again for five minutes and spend them *cutting*. Cut everything you don't like. Chop it down, preserving the bits you do like, but don't add anything at this stage.

Next, set your timer again for another five minutes, and this time you're allowed to write again, but your task is to *rewrite*. You can change anything you like.

Next, set your timer for three minutes. This time your task is to *expand*. Pick something you really like in the work and develop it.

Finally, set your timer for a final five minutes, look at what you've got now, then use all the three editing tools (cutting, rewriting and expanding) to make a piece you're happy with.

Editing makes good writing. First drafts should be a mess of ideas and never the finished article. Your editing skills are your biggest asset – as is your ability and desire to go back and make the work better, better, better. More is more.

# 31st January

*"Life can only be understood backwards;
but must be lived forwards."*
Søren Kierkegaard

**Day Backwards** is Today.

backwards story a write to going are you, task today's for, So.

…this like literally it do to whether choose can You

beginning the with ending and ending the with starting story a tell just Or…

easy ain't backwards writing, Jeez.

luck Good!

# February

# 1st February

*"Creativity is contagious. Pass it on."*
Albert Einstein

Creativity often involves joining the dots between disparate ideas. Your challenge today is to write a piece of prose involving the following six elements. Be imaginative in the way you find the links between them. Enjoy!

- A character with brittle hair.

- A dog toy.

- The line 'Further and further until I couldn't see him any more'.

- A grain of sand.

- A simile of your choice.

- A bright light.

# 2nd February

*"There are no wasted drafts... everything you throw away is
just as valuable as everything you keep."*
Téa Obreht

Today is **Groundhog Day,** a day to revisit the past. But rather than getting stuck in an endless repeating time loop as in the movie, let's use our revisiting for good purpose.

I'd like you to choose a piece of writing you've already worked on, and look at it as if it's new. It needs to be prose with a character in it. Look at the pieces in your notebook so far. Pick your favourite. And give yourself a pat on the back for having some past writing to look back at. What do you like about it? What works? What is redundant?

Now, look at the vocabulary you've used. Search out any boring word and replace it with an exciting one.

Next, look for anything repetitive. Do you use the same word twice? Change one. Are there two lines that essentially say the same thing? Cut one. Is a theme overstated? Slim it down.

Now, we're going to get a bit more radical. What tense is your piece written in and who is speaking? If it's third person ('Ali left their luggage'), change it to first ('I left my luggage') or second ('You left your luggage'). Choose whichever you find most interesting.

Next, change one of the following: the location, the protagonist, or the ending. Try changing the genre. Is it romantic? Rewrite it as a tense thriller. Is it horror? Rewrite it as a book for children.

Take a look at your new versions and compare them to the original. Which do you prefer? Often it's good to get a bit of distance from a piece of writing; it allows you to see it far more clearly. Whenever I have finished a script or a screenplay I put it away for a fortnight and get on with another piece of writing before returning to it – and that fresh-eyed perspective does wonders.

# 3rd February

*"It takes a lot of time to be a genius, you have to sit around so much doing nothing, really doing nothing."*
Gertrude Stein

Today we're going to meditate. WAIT! DON'T RUN AWAY! COME BACK! Just give it a go.

Set your alarm for ten minutes, free yourself from distractions and sit comfortably, cross-legged or on cushions, resting your back against something if you can. Sitting on the floor is good – it grounds you.

Simply sit and concentrate on breathing. If your mind starts to wander, listen to your breathing and use this little mantra to help you. On the in-breath, say silently to yourself 'Let', and on the out-breath 'Go'. When thoughts rise up, don't panic, that's normal. Try picturing a river running along, and any thoughts you have can plop into it and off they go, bye!

Try to switch off and be calm.

When your timer finishes, WELL DONE! You did it!

Now, set your alarm again for another ten minutes, and free-write. See how that ten minutes of calming affects your brain. Free-write anything, capturing on the page whatever comes up for you. Try to write non-stop, writing the word 'rubbish' on repeat if you get stuck. And if that meditation worked for you, try to fit it into your writing routine as a good way to begin a session.

# 4th February

*"Writing a book is an adventure. To begin with it is a toy then an amusement. Then it becomes a mistress, and then it becomes a master, and then it becomes a tyrant and, in the last stage, just as you are about to be reconciled to your servitude, you kill the monster and fling him to the public."*
Winston Churchill

Today you're going to write a pastiche.

Write the beginning (or a midpoint, if you'd rather) of a good, old-fashioned adventure story, set in the 1940s. Your aim is to channel the tone of the period, in order to construct a funny piece that ribs the spirit of that era. It's all bright-eyed intrepid explorers, pilots, captains of sea vessels, swarthy heroes, witty heroines. Pick a protagonist who's swashbuckling, leaps around and says things like 'chaps' and 'chocks away'.

See if you can capture the sense of the period in the descriptions of what they wear, what their goal is and obviously, 'How the devil they speak, old chap! Wrestle that tiger and show him who's the damned hero in this tale, and if you get a lick on, we'll still be home for crumpets!'

# 5th February

*"Creativity takes courage."*
Henri Matisse

The French artist Henri Matisse made beautiful collages by cutting paper into shapes and organising them into patterns. Today, we're going to employ some of the joy of that randomness in our task.

Collect several pages from newspapers or magazines. Cut them into random shapes. About eight pieces is ideal. Put them in an interesting order.

Now, pick one element from each. It could be a colour, a person, a word, a sentence, a headline, a picture of an object. Write down what each of the eight fragments are. These are your story fragments, your ingredients, your map of today's adventure.

Your task is to create something using these fragments, putting them into a new order, as you redesign it for your story. What do you end up with? Random waffle? Or genius? Feel free to write, draw or collage your story today.

# 6th February

*"We will only understand the miracle of life
when we allow the unexpected to happen."*
Paulo Coelho

Today is **National Chopsticks Day**. What I love about using chopsticks is the random nature of what you end up putting in your mouth. More skilled users may not agree, but I often find whatever I was trying to pick up in my poké bowl is quite different from what ends up in my gob.

So, in the spirit of randomness, here we go. If you have a chopstick to hand, great. If you don't, a pencil will do.

Find a book. Open it at random. Twirl the chopstick (or the pencil) in your hand, and allow it to point to a place on the page. Write down the sentence it's pointing at. Then repeat that exercise twice more, so you now have three random sentences.

They are the first, middle and last lines of the piece you're going to write today. The hard version is to use them in the order you picked them. The slightly easier version is if I let you pick the order. I leave it up to you (and your conscience…).

# 7th February

*"Respect your body. Eat well. Dance forever."*
Eliza Gaynor Minden

Happy **National Ballet Day**. Ah, dance. Whether it's ballet, jive or the hula-hula, the freedom we get from movement brings so much joy.

For today's task, I want you to pick a song. It can be absolutely anything. Put it on, turn it up, then dance to it. Do as they do in the saying and 'dance like nobody's watching'. It is *so* fun. And freeing. And it's good for you.

As you dance, think about who else might dance to this song? Where would they be dancing to it? And when? What are the circumstances? Are they alone or being watched? Are they dancing with someone? Is this a life-changing moment for them?

When the song has finished, write them a monologue set before, during or after the moment they dance.

# 8th February

*"I try to build a full personality for each of our cartoon characters – to make them personalities."*
Walt Disney

Have a look through a newspaper or a magazine, and pick two photographs of contrasting-looking people. Draw them as a cartoon, exaggerating their features, giving them an inflated personality: are they *really* angry or *really* posh, *really* old and frail, *really* tall?

The joy of a cartoon is that you make your characters larger than life. Whatever you can glean from the original photographs, push this to the extreme in your drawing. Then write a description underneath of what sort of person this is, and give them a name.

Next, you need to create a scene for these two people. Use one setting, make sure there's a conflict, and give your scene a beginning, a middle and an end. Either draw it as a series of cartoon pictures or write it as dialogue.

FEBRUARY

# 9th February

*"Fiction is such a world of freedom, it's wonderful.
If you want someone to fly, they can fly."*
Alice Walker

Today is **Alice Walker's birthday**. If you haven't read her work, please do. It's nothing short of genius.

For today's task, write the numbers 1 to 50 down the side of your page. Now write a list of your favourite adjectives. I know, fifty is a lot. You might wonder if you know fifty adjectives at all – but I promise you, you do.

And if you run dry, have a flick through a thesaurus and choose some tasty new ones. There are so many fantastic words. From now on, try to use a wider variety in your writing.

I want you to do this because we get far too used to using the same pool of words on repeat. And whilst I don't advocate writing with flowery, descriptive language *at all* – carefully chosen words are better than a multitude – I do think it is worth using a *variety* of words in your prose. Plus, a greater vocabulary will expand your mind and your appreciation of the joys of language. And isn't that enough?

FEBRUARY

# 10th February

"To invent, you need a good imagination and a pile of junk."
Thomas Edison

Pick two well-known stories of your choice, from different genres. Feel free to choose film or television plots. Now pick the protagonist from one, and drop them into the world of the other.

Write that story. What happens if Thomas Hardy's Tess of the d'Urbervilles, an English country girl from the 1890s, walks into Walter White's meth lab in present-day Albuquerque (from *Breaking Bad*)?

# 11th February

*"When it is working, you completely go into another place, you're tapping into things that are totally universal, completely beyond your ego and your own self. That's what it's all about."*

Keith Haring

Going to another place is always an adventure. Today, find a map of the country you live in. Look at some of those place names! I mean... they are *marvellous*. If I look at a map of my bit of the world, the South of England, I might well find myself in Middle Wallop – sounds painful. Or Devizes – sounds scheming. Or Bugs' Bottom – no comment.

From your own map, pick three of the strangest. They are going to become your writing prompts for the day.

Your challenge is to write a piece featuring these three words as follows: one is a location, one is a character name, and one is the wild card, and can feature in your script in any way you choose. For example, it might be the name of a vehicle. A snack. A wonder drug. A hair product. A magical place in the sky.

Try to capture something of the tone of the names in the tone of your writing. A piece set in Pizelli, for example, is likely to be a far stretch stylistically to a tale of Upper Bogtown.

FEBRUARY

# 12th February

It's **Judy Blume's birthday**. How many of our lives were changed by her heroine's teenage trials growing up? 'I must I must increase my bust!' Game-changer.

Today, I would like you to go and buy a magazine that you'd never usually pick up in a million years. A trainspotting magazine? One about caravanning? *The Lady*? *GQ*? A gossip rag? Whatever feels like a leap for you – that's the one.

Have a good look through. Who are the people you see? What kind of people are they? How different are they from those you might normally choose to write about?

Pick a page that you find interesting, find your protagonist, and write a passage inspired by this new world you've discovered. Put yourself in their shoes, be they shiny Christian Louboutins or an old pair of fishing boots.

# 13th February

*"I listen to my old records and I think,
'How did I ever get on the radio?'"*
Dolly Parton

It's **World Radio Day**! So here's a game to celebrate.

Open your notebook, find a pen, and get your radio ready.

Turn it on and write down the first line you hear. Perhaps it's a song lyric. A radio drama. An advert. The news. Whatever it is, write it down. Obviously if it's a piece of music without lyrics then try again. Now, change the station – listen again, and write down the new line.

Do this three more times. You should now have five lines. Your task today is to write something incorporating these five sentences. It could be anything. Maybe it's a radio drama! Go for it, and enjoy the randomness that channel-hopping can bring to the creative process.

# 14th February

*"A girl likes to be crossed a little in love now and then.*
*It is something to think of."*
Jane Austen, *Pride and Prejudice*

It's **Valentine's Day,** and *Pride and Prejudice* is the ultimate romance. Darcy's too proud, Lizzie's too prejudiced (or maybe it's the other way round... depending on perspective) – so they are the last people on earth who'd make a good match. Only... they're not!

The joy of the romcom. The least likely pair end up in love; it's a story as old as you like, but we never seem to tire of it. And the seminal moment in those stories is the unlikely meeting. In movies they call it the 'meet-cute'.

The meet-cute is the moment (often comic) when A meets B. It's often a circumstance that reveals that these two are each other's opposites. It's the meat farmer at the hippy vegetarian rally. The skydive instructor and the man who's terrified of flights. The proud aristocrat who doesn't approve of 'country manners' and the fiercely independent (ahem, prejudiced) girl from a country village, who's so full of her own convictions that she doesn't believe he might be anything other than an arrogant toff.

Your task is to write a list of twenty unlikely couples and the ironic place where they might meet. Then choose one pair and write their meet-cute. They might begin attracted to each other before finding out that they are mortal enemies. Or perhaps they know they're each other's nemesis from the start – yet something happens that ignites a spark. You can write this as a scene or as prose. Up to you. And if you want inspiration, look no further than the genius Nora Ephron, writer of all the best romantic comedies.

# 15th February

*"The most valuable of all talents is that
of never using two words when one will do."*
Thomas Jefferson

Short is good. Succinct is good. And simple can be very good. So here's your task, to practise the idea that less is less.

Take either a page of your own writing from a previous task (I'd recommend this) or choose a long paragraph from a novel.

Now, you're going to replace every word with the simplest alternative you can think of. Choose short words where you had a long one. Replace fancy Latinate or French words, which tend to be long, multisyllabic, often abstract or scientific, with simpler Saxon words which are short, blunt and to the point. Choose 'hen' rather than 'poultry', 'night' rather than 'nocturnal', 'say' not 'proclaim', 'dead' not 'deceased'.

Enjoy stripping the text back to its simplest form – and see whether you find this version more effective.

# 16th February

*"You can't use up creativity.*
*The more you use, the more you have."*
Maya Angelou

Some things in life are defined by the *simplicity* of the pleasure they deliver – and for me, a pancake is one of them.

Not a fancy pancake. Not a multi-stacked, strawberry-crowned American pancake. I am talking about my grandma's old, burnt frying pan, a plastic pot of eggs, flour and milk, and the most rudimentary of pancake toppings… lemon and sugar.

For me, that simple, misshapen lemon-and-sugar-drenched pancake is the food of the gods. It is childhood. My dad rarely cooked, but Pancake Day was one of the rare occasions when he would don an apron. And, though he always set off the smoke alarm and burnt half of them, he did made a mean pancake.

Simple. Lemons juiced in a plastic squeezer, and caster sugar straight out of the bag. Gaily sloshed onto a pancake until it made you wince with the acid kick. Teeth-tingly and glorious.

Around this time of year is **Pancake Day** (aka Shrove Tuesday). I want you to think back and consider what your simple food pleasure is. What is your comfort food? What food do you share with your family that other people might not understand? What secret meal – that would never be cooked for company – brought you together and makes your heart sing to remember it?

Write a paragraph about that experience. Try to include both the sensory experience of eating and the *feeling* that went with it. The ritual of sharing food feeds us in far more ways than simple nutrition.

Then when you're done, read back over it. And maybe go to the kitchen and recreate it for yourself. And maybe stick some in a box and post it to me.

# 17th February

*"All creative people want to do the unexpected."*
Hedy Lamarr

Today is **Random Act of Kindness Day**. So here's your task.

Think of one person in each of the following categories:

1. Someone you know who could do with cheering up, might be lonely or need a little sunshine.

2. Someone who you don't know well, but who contributes to your life... maybe the postman, the people who do the bins, your hairdresser, your kid's teacher.

3. Someone who absolutely won't be expecting to hear from you.

Your task is to write each of these people a postcard. Or a little note. Or a tag attached to a little gift. And get it to them.

There. Wasn't that nice? Make a resolution to send a postcard every month. Put it in your diary. It takes no time at all, but it's a rather life-affirming habit, and who doesn't love getting post?

# 18th February

*"Writing is really a way of thinking – not just feeling but thinking about things that are disparate, unresolved, mysterious, problematic or just sweet."*
Toni Morrison

It's **Toni Morrison's birthday** today. Amongst her many outstanding writerly qualities was her ability to empathise with her heroes, whether they were folks we'd usually feel for or not. It's an essential skill, as she explained to her writing students at Princeton University.

She extolled the virtue of writing from other people's perspective; it helps us to practise empathy and sensitivity, through putting ourselves in someone else's shoes and mindset. She had two favourite exercises to explore this. Pick one of the two and have a go.

Option One: Write a piece about a difficult episode in your own life. However, rather than writing from your own point of view, invent a new person – someone significantly different from you (swap the age, gender, politics, job, etc.). Change the nature of the event to suit this new character, and consider how it might have felt in their shoes, not yours.

Option Two: Think of someone from your past with whom you have had a bad relationship. Someone who you find it hard to feel positive about, who makes you angry or sad. Now write a short story from their perspective, trying to treat them with sympathy.

# 19th February

*"It simply doesn't interest me to write a very simple play.
I don't see why you have to have one simple narrative or line
through. I think if you can have several, why not?
I believe that our brains work that way now... We're used to
listening to two or three things at a time in a way that people
simply weren't in the nineteenth century."*
Timberlake Wertenbaker

It's **Timberlake Wertenbaker's birthday**. Her plays are brilliantly complex and multilayered. There are many ways you can achieve this in the theatre: by writing a cast of characters who span several ideas, themes, places or times. Taking this idea as inspiration today, try this:

Invent a pair of characters from a single past time and place. Pick a specific scenario, e.g. two Victorian explorers in Patagonia, or two nurses in the Crimea. Now, choose another pair of characters in the present day who are in some way linked to your original scenario. Then pick something physical to solidify that link. For example, is your modern scenario set in the same room? Or does the same object appear in both? Or do the characters from both eras have the same job?

Write a dramatic scene for the first pair. There has to be conflict in it. Then write a second scene for your modern characters, which links to your first scene.

Now put the two scenes together, swapping from one to the other. How interesting can you make the links? Is there a mystery in one that is solved in the other? Or an exciting 'reveal', as to how the scenes are related? Or a curious parallel? Can you surprise the audience? Have a go at mashing the two scenes together in different ways (one section of one scene followed by the other in an ABABAB structure, for example), and then try something different (BAB) or both scenes playing simultaneously, lines cutting in and out. How much more fun is this than a regular scene?!

# 20th February

*"Wanting to be someone else
is a waste of the person you are."*
Kurt Cobain

On musician **Kurt Cobain's birthday,** let's take inspiration from his quote. Today your task is to write about:

*A time you learnt a life lesson.*

Something that made you appreciate the person that you are. Because you are great. You know that, right?

# 21st February

*"There are two different ways to approach writing.
The first is engineered. This approach is more mathematical
and focuses on structure. These writers like to know
everything that is going to happen before they start writing.
The second way is to follow your instinct.
I have always felt closer to the second path."*
Elif Shafak

Today you're going to write about an experience – but *only* using the narrator's sense of smell. You're not going to tell us anything about the place – what it looks like, when it is, what's happening, what you can hear, who's narrating… describing the smell is your *one* way of telling this story. Think about the order of smells, the pungency, the strength, the softness, the speed of the aromas beginning or intensifying. Are they pleasant? Are they surprising? How do they shift?

It'll be easier if you pick a scenario in which smell – pleasant or otherwise – might feature specifically. Perhaps a hospital, a restaurant or a chemistry lab.

How can you substitute all your normal storytelling tools with only this one sense? Sounds impossible, but you might surprise yourself.

# 22nd February

*"Keep good company, read good books, love good things."*
Louisa May Alcott

Today we are in writer-training mode. Think of yourself as a word athlete, and we're going to do a HIIT class. For those of you fortunate never to have been to one, HIIT stands for 'High Intensity Interval Training' and it's basically short, sharp and *painful*. Quick reps of short exercises that leave your arms and legs feeling like blancmange that hasn't set properly.

Here are today's much more enjoyable HIIT exercises, which will get your writing muscles activated.

Set a timer and do each of the following for *two minutes* each, writing as many words in each category as you can in the time:

1.  Write a list of adjectives (descriptive words) beginning with 'G' (gracious, glorious, gorgeous, galumphing…).

2.  Write a list of boys' names beginning with 'A'.

3.  Write a list of verbs (doing words) beginning with 'F' (fling, fart, furrow…).

4.  Write a list of words associated with birds.

5.  Write a list of brilliant words! (Words that fill you with joy when you say them, either because of the sounds, or because you enjoy the meaning: 'phantasmagoria', for example, as a word that is fun to say, or 'sunshine' for its meaning.)

6.  Write a list of all the colours you can think of.

# 23rd February

*"She reads books as one would breath air, to fill up and live."*
Annie Dillard

Today we're going to celebrate the limitless potential of storytelling. Of all the different possibilities that can fly out when you open the door at the beginning of a tale.

I'm going to give you the first line of your story and you are going to complete it, by writing or drawing what happens next. Then, using the same first line, I'd like you to write or draw an alternative end to the sentence. Then again. Then again, until you have completed this first line in ten different ways.

The game is to make them as radically different from each other as possible. What different types of story might this be? And if you love one in particular, why not pursue the idea and create a whole scene?

So, your starter line is:

Martha waited for the doors to open – and when they did…

# 24th February

*"I am my own experiment. I am my own work of art."*
Madonna

Pick a country, any country.

Now pick a name from the following: Manuella, Ali, Bob, Fandango, Mrs Scrogg, Peach, Stuart Allen Gorballic, Mr Lovatt, Pip, Finbar.

Now pick a second name from the list.

Pick a location from the following: A restaurant kitchen, a pottery factory, a treehouse, a bird hide, a cellar, a veterinary surgery, a candlemaker's studio.

You've guessed it. These are the ingredients for today's piece of writing. Put these two characters in your location in the country of choice and see what happens. And one final ingredient: someone has just been born. That person isn't one of your two characters – it happens outside the room – but knowledge of it feeds your scenario. You can write in prose or dialogue.

# 25th February

*"Every grain of experience is food
for the greedy growing soul of the artist."*
Anthony Burgess

Everything around us is food for our imaginations. We need to grab it all and stuff it in our mouths like insatiable teenagers.

Today, go for a walk outside, find someone interesting to observe, take a pew and start watching them. Obviously, do this courteously and discreetly, your job is to observe, not to make anyone uncomfortable!

Write down everything you notice about them. What they wear, how they move, what they notice, what speed they are going, what their motivation seems to be, how they seem emotionally. Who do they interact with? How?

Then continue your walk and find a second person to observe, and repeat the exercise. Make sure this person doesn't have anything to do with your first person.

Now, put together a scenario involving these two characters and a meeting of some sort – and write it.

Finally, be pleased that all your work today was inspired by the world around you – it is physically impossible that you could have written this piece yesterday, or in any other location. Drawing on observations in the present is an effective way to keep your writing fresh. Unlike drawing solely on memory and personal experience, using the surprising and unpredictable world around you as a starting point means you'll never run out of inspiration.

FEBRUARY

# 26th February

*"Fairytales do not tell children the dragons exist.*
*Children already know that dragons exist.*
*Fairytales tell children the dragons can be killed."*
G. K. Chesterton

Today is **National Tell a Fairytale Day**. But why? Let's have a think about why these stories get told over and over – and it's not *just* because Disney created sexy foxes and good songs about very cold sisters.

Fairytales endure because they are deeply moral tales about the struggle between good and bad (Snow White and the Evil Queen, Hansel and Gretel versus the Witch, the greedy Wolf who tempts Red Riding Hood), in which foolishness or bad traits are punished (liars' noses grow, overly curious women fall asleep for ages, silly old people get eaten by wolves). And they always have big satisfying endings where there's at the very least a big party, a wedding and a dead giant.

But… a lot of them are dated. So today you're going to pick a fairytale and do a twist on it. You could modernise it, setting it now. You could write a revisionist version in which young women with curiosity aren't punished for it, but win after all (hoorah – about time!). Or you can rewrite the tale from a new perspective; from the point of view of one of the dwarves, or the mirror that gets broken, or Rapunzel's long, long hair. Make it your own.

Here are a few tales to choose from, or pick your own:

- 'Snow White and the Seven Dwarves'
- 'Sleeping Beauty'
- 'Cinderella'
- 'Red Riding Hood'
- 'Jack and the Beanstalk'
- 'Rapunzel'
- 'The Gingerbread Man'
- 'Rumpelstiltskin'

# 27th February

*"Ideas are like rabbits. You get a couple and learn how to handle them, and pretty soon you have a dozen."*
John Steinbeck

Well, look at that – today is **John Steinbeck's birthday**, one of my favourite writers… and my birthday too! I feel honoured.

So, to honour the great man, let's take one of his top writing tips as a jumping-off point. Steinbeck suggested that, whenever you are writing dialogue, you must say it aloud as you write it. It's a tip I stand by. As a playwright I am constantly muttering to myself as I write, speaking the lines out loud and editing as I go to make sure every line sounds like real speech. It's amazing how speaking lines out loud tells you instinctively whether it sounds authentic or not. And it's a mistake many beginner writers make in the theatre… writing pages of dialogue with sentences far more cumbersome or expositional than a real person would ever utter, and then wondering why their scripts end up in the reject pile.

So let's not do that. Today, you're going to write a brilliant script. Only one character, making a speech. And, because it's my birthday, as my gift to you, you can write whatever you like! A character stands to make a speech to an audience they have to win over, but who they are and what the context is are entirely up to you. Go for it. It can be anything. And as you write it, speak it *as you go*. Not when the whole thing is finished, but as you write each line.

You may be amazed what a difference it makes.

# 28th February

Today is **National Science Day** – so I want you to pick an incredible scientific invention or discovery. The easiest and most fun way is to google exactly that. The wacky things that come up will blow your mind and are infinitely more ridiculous than you would invent yourself. Trust me, I just tried it and the first result was 'sixty-six-million-year-old "Wonder chicken" becomes oldest known modern bird'. It's actually a good story.

Do your research. Pick your invention, then write it into a dramatic scenario. A scene for a play rather than prose, so it needs to be dialogue. Keep the number of characters small, so that you can relish the intimacy of the discovery being made, as the consequences are revealed. Where is the drama in it? Try to add some extra spice. Is there a revelation? Might one of the characters try to take credit for this discovery? Or is there a dark side to the invention that only becomes apparent as the scene progresses? Exciting!

# 29th February

*"It takes three springs to make one leap year."*
The Comic Almanack, c. 1852

Ooh a **Leap Day**! If there's a 29th February in the year you're reading this, what a win, an extra day! Quick – leap to it, take advantage, it's a gift!

I love leap days. They feel like they exist between the folds of regular time, like a snippet of extra life that we shouldn't rightly get… That's why it feels like something magical might happen.

H. G. Wells evidently felt the same, judging by the opening he wrote to *The Invisible Man*. And as a hat-tip to him, we're going to borrow his first line and use it as the first line of today's story. After you've written or drawn your own, maybe go and see what he did with his. It's astonishing.

Begin your story, as he did, with:

> 'So it was that on the twenty-ninth day of February, at the beginning of the thaw, this singular personal fell out of infinity into Iping Village…'

F E B R U A R Y

# March

# 1st March

*"A good poem is a contribution to reality.
The world is never the same once a good poem has been
added to it. A good poem helps to change the shape of the
universe, helps to extend everyone's knowledge of himself
and the world around him."*
Dylan Thomas

Today is **St David's Day**, patron saint of Wales, land of my particular forefathers, and the home of one of our greatest poets, Dylan Thomas. Many of my childhood days were spend squelching in the mud in the estuary in Laugharne, where Thomas's writing boathouse was perched, as we stuck our arms into the sinking sand, looking for lugworms.

Today, in honour of a country of beautiful landscapes, and a poet who wrote about nature like no other, your task is to write a nature poem. But I want you to use sound *within* words to create a descriptive feast for the mouth. Thomas loved the *sound* of words. At the beginning of *Under Milk Wood,* he describes the '*moonless night in the small town, starless and bible-black, the cobblestreets silent and the hunched, courters'- and- rabbits' wood limping invisible down to the sloeblack, slow, black, crowblack, fishingboat-bobbing sea.*'

Read this paragraph out loud. Listen to the repeated vowel sounds: 'slow', 'sloe', 'crow'. And the plosive 'b' sounds: 'sloeback', 'black', 'crowblack', 'boat-bobbing'.

Now, either go outside or think of a place in nature that means something to you, that evokes particular feelings. And write a poetic poem, describing nature, using the sounds of language as your canvas. Look out for opportunities to rhyme, to alliterate, to enjoy the mouth muscles at work.

Then go and read some more Thomas poetry. It's a joy.

# 2nd March

*"The first duty of the novelist is to entertain. It is a moral duty. People who read your books are sick, sad, travelling, in the hospital waiting room while someone is dying. Books are written by the alone for the alone."*
Donna Tartt

It's amazing how much joy you can get from reading, right? So today, simply return to one of your favourite books – something that you really enjoyed – and re-read a particularly excellent section. Read it for pleasure, but also with an eye to what you find so wonderful about the writing. Write down three of your favourite lines. That's it. Savour and enjoy them.

MARCH

# 3rd March

*"Each letter of the alphabet is a steadfast loyal soldier in
a great army of words, sentences, paragraphs and stories.
One letter falls, and the entire language falters."*
Vera Nazarian

The world is full of excellent words. Fibrous words; delicious words; zingy words; lugubrious words. Today's exercise is to write out the alphabet, A to Z, and to think of a fantastic adjective beginning with each letter; for example, Artful, Bromidic, Cogent, Dapper…

Double points if you find one for every letter of the alphabet.

MARCH

# 4th March

*"Visions are worth fighting for.*
*Why spend your life making someone else's dreams?"*
Scott Alexander and Larry Karaszewski, *Ed Wood*

Orson Welles believed wholeheartedly in making the work that *he* believed in, not what the movie studios wanted him to make. *His* dreams.

It doesn't always make for an easy career, but being authentic is a key part of finding happiness and fulfilment as a writer. Rather than trying to write something you think will be popular, or follow the zeitgeist (never a good idea… it will have changed utterly before you have finished your manuscript), have faith in your own voice. What is *your* experience? What do *you* find interesting?

Today, write a list of ten things you would dream of writing about. That you'd like to write for *your own pleasure*, ignoring any notion of what you think might be popular. Imagine a publisher/producer/ theatre company said to you: 'Here's a cheque, you can write anything you like…' What would it be?

Think back through your own life. Are there moments you'd like to dramatise? Or is it stepping imaginatively into someone else's experience which excites you? What sort of work do you love to read? Is that your genre? Who would be your ideal hero/heroine? Who do you *really* want to write about?

# 5th March

*"I love deadlines.
I love the whooshing noise they make as they go by."*
Douglas Adams

Pressure is good for characters. Stuff happens when the pressure gauge is turned up, when the mercury rises, when the walls begin closing in.

Today, pick a character, any character, either from your own existing work or from someone else's. Now, think of their nemesis. Who would they least like to be stuck with if they got trapped somewhere?

And that's what we're going to do. Choose your confined space and write a short story or scene in which your two characters end up stuck. It's Lizzie Bennet and Darcy stuck in Hannah's cleaning closet downstairs at Longbourn. It's Luke Skywalker and Darth Vader stuck inside the exhaust port of the Death Star with no escape.

What happens now? Do they battle it out? Do they have to work together to escape? Does only one of them get out? Do they realise, having been forced into this close encounter, that they have misunderstood each other and are actually... wildly in love? Or related? Anything's possible.

MARCH

# 6th March

*"Inspiration is some mysterious blessing which happens when the wheels are turning smoothly."*
Quentin Blake

Today you're going to take inspiration from what's in front of you. From wherever you are sitting, have a good look around and pick one random object. Try to find something with some personality.

From my seat in the kitchen, for example, I can currently see:

- A tall, plastic electric fan with spokes that looks like a smug face.

- A bottle of nearly neon Amalfi orange gin, half drunk, bringing a ray of Italian sunshine into our South London flat.

- And Fezzer, the tattered furry pheasant toy that my dog, Newt, has loved until it's nearly shredded.

Each of these objects has a story to tell. And today's exercise is to write from the point of view of one of them. If I were writing as Fezzer, for example, I'm sure I'd be sick of being used as Newt's tooth cleaner. However, today we bought Newt a new toy, a garish purple elephant, hence why Fezzer has been abandoned on the kitchen floor. Perhaps he is secretly envious.

What can you see? What will their story be? Create this story either in writing or as a series of images.

# 7th March

*"The desire to reach the stars is ambitious.
The desire to reach hearts is wise and most possible."*
Maya Angelou

To begin today's task, write a list of all the character traits that you most dislike in a person. Get them all out. You know – those *really* annoying things other people do that fill you with rage. Or disgust. Or make you huff like an old grump.

Me personally, I hate it when people have indiscreet conversations loudly on their phones in public. I get embarrassed for them and wish to God they would stop! Or that there'd be a momentary phone-signal crash or *anything*, but *please* stop talking about why your neighbour's sister's niece is pregnant again.

I also hate queue-jumpers.

Write your list. Make it specific – as it's the detail of the flaws that give you material. Let's face it, we all hate racists, misogynists, bullies, people who kick puppies and put kittens in bins. But try to be original and specific in your choice of pet peeves.

Once you have a few good traits – three or four should be enough – they will be the building blocks for today's character. This protagonist has *all* these bad habits. Who is this terrible person? Why are they like that? And what happens to them? Perhaps, ironically, it is these flaws that endear them to us.

Write a passage about your character. Take them on a journey, put them in a compromising situation and see if you can carve out a way to see them as a hero. Who knows, perhaps this has been the cheapest therapy session and you'll never be annoyed by these things ever again?

# 8th March

Today you're going to write down a list of all the words that have a physical effect on you, words that make you *feel* something. Most people will find that the sound of certain words makes you relax (in my case, 'mellifluous'), squirm ('nip') or laugh ('bonk').

Your task is very simple – there's no need to write down why, but have a go at brainstorming every word that inspires a physical reaction, and what that response is.

MARCH

# 9th March

*"When inspiration does not come, I go for a walk, go to the movie, talk to a friend, let go... The muse is bound to return again, especially if I turn my back!"*
Judy Collins

Let's take some inspiration from the outside world today. Like Judy Collins says, if the muse doesn't come knocking, go out and find them.

Today you're going to use a newspaper headline as a prompt for a story. And then write an original article, inspired entirely by the headline, not the same story as the actual article. This is your chance to be wildly imaginative and make it up completely.

In an ideal world, wander to your local independent corner shop and pick a headline from one of the papers. The more attention-grabbing but abstract it is, the better: 'London stock market drops four points' is *not* what we are after. Better are titles that could mean anything, such as these excellent puns (which you're welcome to borrow if you're not up for going to the shop):

- 'I've been Edam Fool'

- 'Fizzy Pope'

- 'Between Iraq and a Hard Place'

- 'Ant and Decked'

- 'Wagatha Christie Returns'

- 'Algorithm and Blues'

- 'Tea and Antipathy'

# 10th March

*"I paint flowers so they will not die."*
Frida Kahlo

Let's talk about titles. I know, I know... you may not have written the book yet, but maybe the chicken came before the egg, who knows?

So here we go. Find a picture of an interesting scene – a photo in a newspaper, or a random image search online. Have a good look at it. Who is in it? What's the action? What intrigues you about it? What's its tone?

This photo is going to be the front cover of your book. And now you have to come up with a title for the novel. Try each of the following (I've done some examples based on a photograph of two kids pond-dipping for newts):

- Write a long, literal title that explains exactly what's happening (*A boy and a girl lie in the sun, at a pond's edge, trying to catch newts*).

- Write a title that is the brightest and most positive (*Glimmers on the Water*).

- Write a tragic title (*The Drowning*).

- Write a one-word title that is literal (*Pond-dipping*).

- Write a one-word title that might be a pun or have a second meaning (*The Dipper*).

- Write a title that captures the mood of the picture (*Summer Song*).

- Write a title lifted from a poem or song (*Where the Rocking Billows Rise and Sink*).

- Write the naffest title (*Newts, Roots and Sunshine Fruits*).

- Write a title inspired by the location (*The Water's Edge*).

- Write a title using the character names (*Frank and Gwen*).

- Write a title that makes no sense (*The Wonders of Ice Cream*).

- Write a completely pretentious title (*Upon a Watery Bower*).

- Steal a title from an existing novel that might work (*Loss of Innocence*).

- Write a title that gives the end away (*The Break-up*).

- Write a romcom title (*Meet-Newt*).

- Write a title from the perspective of the photographer (*Three's a Crowd*).

- Write a title with a sense of anticipation (*Before the Rains Came*).

- Write a good title! And then the book...

# 11th March

*"I don't think there's any artist of any value
who doesn't doubt what they're doing."*
Francis Ford Coppola

Today, you need a box of matches. You are going to strike a match, and within the time that it takes to burn out, tell a scary story. When the match fizzles out (or when you're about to burn your fingers!) – that's it, time's up.

How was it? Hard? Did you say anything remotely interesting or scary? Or were you just rushing? Yup. You rushed.

Now try again, but this time: say less. Your job is to create atmosphere. Jump into the story when it's already dramatic. And leave us hanging with a mystery ending. Did it work?

A bit?

So try again. This time try to create drama and tension but go slooooow. Maybe your whole story is only a single line. Better, right?

Now, one more time: only single words. Say. Very. Little. Leave. Us. Wanting…?

Try one last time, using whatever you've learnt. No doubt it'll be so much better than your original attempt.

The economy of expression is a very powerful thing. Now write out your version of your ghost story, using this new superpower. I'll bet it's a winner.

# 12th March

*"Great things are not accomplished by those who yield to trends and fads and popular opinion."*
Jack Kerouac

Happy birthday **Jack Kerouac**, quite a character. Here he describes his daily routine, which became more prescriptive, superstitious and obsessive as he aged:

> *'I had a ritual once of lighting a candle and writing by its light and blowing it out when I was done for the night […] also kneeling and praying before starting (I got that from a French movie about George Frideric Handel) […] but now I simply hate to write. My superstition? I'm beginning to suspect the full moon. Also I'm hung up on the number nine though I'm told a Piscean like myself should stick to number seven; but I try to do nine touchdowns a day, that is, I stand on my head in the bathroom, on a slipper, and touch the floor nine times with my toe tips, while balanced. This is incidentally more than yoga, it's an athletic feat, I mean imagine calling me 'unbalanced' after that. Frankly I do feel that my mind is going. So another 'ritual' as you call it, is to pray to Jesus to preserve my sanity and my energy so I can help my family: that being my paralyzed mother, and my wife, and the ever-present kitties. Okay?'*

Yes, okay, Jack. You do you.

Your task today is to write about someone who has *very* specific rituals in their day – and what happens when something prevents them from doing them. Obsession is a great character trait. Have fun with inventing some for your character. And the more they *have* to do them, the greater the drama when they can't.

For example, might your character do fifty star-jumps while the kettle boils in the morning? What does that say about them?

Or do they always peep on their neighbour as he does yoga in his conservatory... until the day when they see – what? Ooh, there's a story.

Or might she always kiss her signet ring before operating on patients? And yet, when she's about to start the operation on the conjoined twins, our surgeon discovers that her ring has disappeared?

# 13th March

*"The first draft is just you telling yourself the story."*
Terry Pratchett

Today's task may make you feel uncomfortable, as you're going to write in the second person – i.e. addressing the protagonist as 'you' (e.g. 'You were walking along the tightrope…').

We so often write in the first person or the third. The second feels weird. It suddenly oddly implicating or intimate.

So your exercise today is to simply write for ten minutes in the second person. Choose your tense. Perhaps try the present tense: 'You are trying to push through the crowd, when the woman in green ducks behind a pillar. She's gone.' To write in the present tense feels *very* odd, though it has an element of immediacy, placing the reader in the action, which can be interesting when used sparingly.

Or try the past tense, as if you're addressing the 'you'. You can think of this as a letter, as used brilliantly in *We Need to Talk About Kevin* by Lionel Shriver: 'You went into school and did a terrible thing.'

Just have a go. Mix things up. See what happens.

# 14th March

*"Writing books is the closest men ever come to childbearing."*
Norman Mailer

If today is a Sunday and you're in the UK, it may well be **Mother's Day**, since it almost always falls in March. If so, Happy Mother's Day! But even if it isn't, or if you're in a country with a different Mother's Day, let's use today to delve into the theme of mums and motherhood. Whether you know your mother well, whether you're close or not, doesn't matter here – you simply need to be able to describe her. And if you don't have a mother – perhaps you have two dads, for example – pick on or a similar figure in your life. Someone who has been a guardian or guide, whether they're a relation or not.

Set your timer for four minutes and write a list of every detail you can about this person. Their appearance, personality, traits, skills, flaws, habits, pet peeves, everything.

When the timer goes off, look at your list.

Now you're going to go through the list and write, in a new list, the opposite of each thing you wrote down. Is your mum broad? Write 'waifish'. Is she tidy? Write 'messy'. You get the picture.

This list is going to be your character outline for the mother in today's scenario – someone who's diametrically opposite to your own mum. Put this new mum into a dramatic scene, with one other person and some sort of conflict. A handy hint: pick one of her flaws to inspire the source of a conflict in the scene.

And write the scene. Enjoy!

# 15th March

*"Intoxicated? The word did not express it by a mile. He was oiled, boiled, fried, plastered, whiffled, sozzled, and blotto."*
P. G. Wodehouse, *Meet Mr. Mulliner*

Happy **National Word Day!** There are so many brilliant, vivid words in the world – sometimes it's fun to use them. Often when writing, the simplest vocabulary is the best, but not today. So get that thesaurus out and start enjoying yourself.

You're going to write the first paragraph of a story. Pick a place, ideally somewhere with lots of sensory stimulation. A meat-packing factory. A tea plantation. A chaotic operating theatre. Now make a list, for all five senses, of everything you can conjure up about the place. Make sure you use all of them: smell, taste, sound, touch, sight. When you've come up with your basic list, go back and add an abstract idea into each sense list. For example, the smell of decay is literal – but what is the *feeling* of that smell? The smell of fear? Of your turning gut? Of a mouldy yellow?

Now, go to the thesaurus and find some of the words in your paragraph, then pick your favourite synonyms on the list. Perhaps, in the meat factory, you wrote the word 'rotting' for the leftover meat. In the thesaurus you might find 'putrid', 'fetid', 'malodorous', 'rank', 'reeking', 'mouldered'... all great words! I want you to use them all.

For inspiration, let's look at the opening from one of my very favourite books (if you haven't read it, you have an absolute joy in store), John Steinbeck's remarkable *Cannery Row*. In terms of knowing how to use vocabulary to drop us straight into the landscape, there's no one more masterful than Steinbeck. You can smell the sardines. Enjoy, take note, and off you go!

*'Cannery Row in Monterey in California is a poem, a stink, a grating noise, a quality of light, a tone, a habit, a nostalgia, a dream.*

*Cannery Row is the gathered and scattered, tin and iron and rust and splintered wood, chipped pavement and weedy lots and junk heaps, sardine canneries of corrugated iron, honky tonks, restaurants and whore houses, and little crowded groceries, and laboratories and flophouses. Its inhabitant are, as the man once said, "whores, pimps, gambler and sons of bitches," by which he meant Everybody. Had the man looked through another peephole he might have said, "Saints and angels and martyrs and holymen" and he would have meant the same thing.'*

# 16th March

*"It was all so far away – there was quiet and an untouched feel to the country and I could work as I pleased."*
Georgia O'Keeffe

Sit by a window and wait for someone to walk by. Someone interesting… not necessarily the first person that passes. When they do, take in as much detail about that person as you can. How do they move? What are they doing? Where might they be going? What do you imagine they might be like?

Now you're going to write a short scenario about what happens to them when they get home. Where do they live? With whom? What happens when they arrive? What could the drama be? Make sure there *is* drama.

If you don't live somewhere that anyone's likely to walk past, then head on out and find a spot where you can see some passers-by. A café, a station, a bus stop, a park bench. Only if you live so remotely that you've got no hope of seeing another human for days – if you work as a solo Arctic researcher at a polar station, for example – should you use the back-up method: switch on the TV and pick a person that appears on the screen *or* type something random into Google, have a look at the first people who come up and pick one. But that's the only reason to not to do this in person; avoid using a screen if you can.

# 17th March

*"Chick lit uses humour to reflect life back to us.
It's a very comforting genre, and it's the first time our
generation has had a voice. It's a very important genre for all
of those reasons."*
Marian Keyes

Chick lit... love it or hate it, you can't argue with the fact that it's a genre that often cleverly bends the narrative to intertwine characters' stories for emotional impact. Popular writers like Cecelia Ahern, Sophie Kinsella, Ernessa T. Carter and Virginia DeBerry often play these sort of narrative games. Separate characters in separate narratives have some link that is only revealed later in the book. They're sisters, perhaps! Or one has the other's heart. Or they lived in the same house. Their stories collide across time or location. So today, inspired by such twisty works of fiction, we're going to swing away from the convention of linear storytelling and make our own multilayered narrative.

First, I want you to pick a location in a public place, where you'd find a seat. A pew in a church, for example. A stump in a cemetery, a bench on a canal path or an old tyre swing in a woodland.

Now, draw a picture of your place – and imagine who might be found on this seat at sunrise. Is it someone on their own? Perhaps there are a pair of people? Do they arrange to meet there? You're going to write a paragraph about this moment: the person (or people) at the seat and what happens there.

Now, imagine winding the clock forward to some time later that day – you choose when. Repeat the exercise, considering who you might find at the seat at this time and write that paragraph.

Now, for part three, wind the clock forward to the darkness of night. Who's there now and what are they doing?

Next, re-read all three and think of a way to tie them together, to make the characters' lives intertwine. How do they link? Do they know each other? Do the people have something in common? Is the experience of the later sitters affected by something the earlier people did, or left at the seat, perhaps?

The last part of the exercise is to write a final paragraph that somehow reveals the link between them. There you go: you have a multilayered story right there.

MARCH

# 18th March

*"I've gone through the village of my songwriting and my artistry, and I've gone through lots of different phases, including one where it has been very quiet and abandoned me for a few years."*
Carly Simon

You know when that cringey awkward thing happens that you know you're going to remember for your whole life. Yeah, that.

Today – **National Awkward Moments Day** (no, I didn't make it up) – it's time to take it out of the dark place you've hidden it because it's a simple writing-prompt day – and your task is to write about:

That *incident*.

Good luck. And don't worry, no one can see you blushing.

# 19th March

*"I'm always pretending that I'm sitting across from somebody. I'm telling them a story, and I don't want them to get up until it's finished."*
James Patterson

If you're going to write every day, it's good to train yourself to write anywhere. It's all very well creating your perfect writing space, with your favourite candle, view, secret snack drawer... (oh yes, I know). But we are so frequently *not* in our regular spaces or routines that you'd do well to get good at writing wherever you happen to be.

I write on the bus. On the Tube. Sometimes on a dirty bench at a Tube station as I'm halfway through writing an idea and I'm determined to finish before I get to where I'm going. I write at the lido while the swimmers splash about, I've even written in the bath. I mean... without any water in it, but sharing a room with a friend who goes to bed before me has, sometimes, necessitated typing away in the bathroom till the small hours in the only place with available light.

So today, your challenge is to write a short story in three parts. A beginning, middle and end. And physically write each part in a different place – *none* of which should be in your house. Challenge yourself to write in places that feel transitory, that aren't idyllic writing spots. Don't go to a hushed library. Write at a bus stop. Or in a loud greasy spoon. Get used to parking yourself wherever you happen to be on the journey of your day and write there. It's a great benefit to be able to work anywhere – you get so much more done!

# 20th March

*"Experiment. Play. Make us laugh, and then make us cry."*
A. M. Homes

Today, let's do a writing game. You're going to write a piece of prose in which you use the SOUND of the letter of the alphabet in order: Ay, Be, See, Dee, Ee, Eff, etc. They don't have to begin the sentences, or even begin words – you just need to sneak them into your prose.

For example, your first line could be something like:

'M*AY*be I should have read the sign *BE*fore I jumped. But I don't remember *SEE*ing it, I was so caught up in the *DE*light of doing something spontaneous. And no one stopped m*E*. So I jumped…'

The sounds of the letters will give you a fun map to follow when you're writing, and might bend your story in a direction that you wouldn't expect. Enjoy!

For inspiration, check out Tim Minchin's brilliant 'School Song' in *Matilda the Musical*, where he does exactly that.

# 21st March

It's **World Poetry Day** today – so, of course, it's time to write a poem. But where to start? Let's do one of the oldest writerly tricks in the book… Steal an idea. Though we'll call it 'inspiration'.

I'd like you to choose a poem that has a specific format and write your own version. Take the layout and theme of the poem but write it to make it personal to you. Pay attention to the structure of the poem: is there a rhyme scheme, and if so how does it work? What is the central idea, and how to does it get introduced, unpacked and concluded? What is the tone of the poem? Is it tongue-in-cheek, serious or funny?

Here are some potential poems to use – I've picked them for their specific forms that take an idea and deconstruct it in a poetic fashion. Start by reading all five examples (all are available on the internet), they're all exceptional – then pick one, or choose your own:

- 'Phenomenal Woman' by Maya Angelou

- 'What a poem is not' by John Hegley

- 'Valentine (My Love is Like an Onion)' by Carol Ann Duffy

- 'I Wanna Be Yours' by John Cooper Clarke

- 'Social Distancing' by Juan Felipe Herrera

# 22nd March

*"If people have split views about your work,
I think it's flattering. I'd rather have them feel something
about it than dismiss it."*
Stephen Sondheim

Well said, Mr Sondheim! One of the worst pitfalls as you begin to write is write to please other people. It means you'll write what you *think* other people want – which they probably won't, because good writing is original with an authentic voice. As soon as you fall into the trap of trying to please others, or write what you think is commercial, you'll end up mimicking something that someone else has already done, sooner and better than you.

So follow your heart. Use your own voice and worry not one jot about what anyone else thinks. Today's task is to write a list of all the things that mean something to you. Yes, that sounds like a huge question – it is! So embrace it. What do you care about? What issues? What places? Who? Which objects? What music? What ideas? What priorities?

Take ten minutes writing a list (set a timer), then take a look at it and see if you can distil it into a list of principles. How are you defined by your interests and passions? And what story or genre of story does that guide you towards?

# 23rd March

*"Youth is wasted on the young."*
George Bernard Shaw

Today, write a letter to your younger self. Pick a time when you think you could have done with hearing from your new older and wiser self... When were things difficult? When did you worry unnecessarily? When did you think you'd never get through a tricky time? What would you say to reassure your younger self? What advice would you give yourself? What would you have liked to hear?

Write with kindness and compassion. And maybe think about what you had then that you didn't appreciate – how good things really were; what you miss now about that time (if anything); and why it's important to embrace those parts of life, people or things you didn't realise were quite so precious at the time.

MARCH

# 24th March

*"If you were to say to me that I couldn't paint, I would write.
If I couldn't write, I would be a set designer.
As long as I'm creating something, I'm happy."*
Grace Slick

In an unusual break from the conventions of this book, today's exercise is a continuation – or a response to – yesterday's. Yesterday I asked you to write a letter to your younger self, giving yourself some life advice and reminding you to appreciate what you had then – and to be reassured that, whatever you were finding tricky, you'd come out the other side, thriving.

For today's exercise, I want you to imagine yourself either ten or twenty years in the future and write a letter from the future to your present-day self. Consider what you are dealing with in life now. What is challenging? What sometimes feels overwhelming? How are you too hard on yourself? Write from the fictional future to tell your current self why you shouldn't worry. Remind yourself of all the great qualities that you have right now – including your youth! And how you'll likely be looking back thinking how great you were and how much you didn't realise at the time... as Baz Luhrmann brilliantly reminds us in his fantastic song 'Everybody's Free (To Wear Sunscreen)', which is well worth revisiting (you can find it on YouTube). 'You are not as fat as you think you are.'

Enjoy the chance to write this letter. Essentially, it's a self-appreciation piece and a reminder that you are, in fact, fabulous, and you should celebrate that fact. Because, frankly, it's true.

# 25th March

*"As the story grew, it put down roots into the past and threw out unexpected branches."*
J. R. R. Tolkien, *The Fellowship of the Ring*

Today we're going to write with constraints. It's a really good way to challenge yourself to write differently.

You're going to write a story with the following structure: Your first sentence has to have three words. The next five. The next seven. The next one. The next nine. Then repeat the same structure again. Then continue writing, but every sentence *must* contain an odd number of words, and your final four sentences must have, in order, seven, five, three then one word in them only.

Read back over your story and see which sentences you like the most. How have you challenged your usual form? How did it make you approach storytelling differently? Which lines are most effective?

# 26th March

*"When I stop working the rest of the day is posthumous.
I'm only really alive when I'm writing."*
Tennessee Williams

Today is **Tennessee Williams' birthday**. A playwright of tremendous emotional depth and devastating storytelling, he often used memory as a tool in his writing.

In addition to drawing on his memories for plot, he also experimented with memory as form. In *The Glass Menagerie*, for example, Tom sets himself up as an unreliable narrator by telling the audience that this is 'a memory play' – in other words, it's his version of what happened. We are seeing through a filter, through his eyes, only what he remembers, which is just one version of the truth. He tells us:

> *'The play is memory. Being a memory play, it is dimly lighted, it is sentimental, it is not realistic. In memory everything seems to happen to music. That explains the fiddle in the wings. I am the narrator of the play, and also a character in it.'*

Your task today is to write a scene from your own life as a scene from a memory play. You have licence to make it 'dimly lighted' and 'sentimental'. How can you add poetry to the reality of what happened? How do you paint the characters as interesting stage presences? Think about music, symbolism, speech that you can elevate to be more poetic, deeply emotional, to create something compelling and beautiful.

Then, try writing the same scene again with the lyricism stripped away, a realistic 'kitchen sink' version, which plays as close to the truth as possible. Which is more effective? And which did you prefer to write?

# 27th March

*"Everything influences playwrights. A playwright who isn't influenced is never of any use."*
Arthur Miller

Today, write a list of all the people who've influenced you. Start from the very beginning. Who's the first person you remember inspiring you? Was it a teacher? An eccentric auntie? Someone's parent? Your mum or dad? An older kid at school? Who did you look at and glow?

The first person I remember to give me that 'glow' was a wool-wrapped, cherry-faced warm hug of a woman, who held group 'musical classes' for the under-fives at her yellow-brick cottage in Twyford. She'd let us stick our hands inside the piano and touch the moving parts as she played. She'd get us banging on pots, playing animal characters as we made up improvised songs to her guitar accompaniment, and she always, *always* had milk and pink wafers for us at break time. I can't quite remember her face. She's now a blur in my memory – more of a presence, an outline – but what I do remember vividly is the thrill of her classes, and I walked away with a love of music that has never left me.

Make your list. Do it chronologically, so you can work through the periods of your life and scan them for inspiring people. Then pick one person from your list and write why. Describe them, and how they made you feel, what they did and how it has stayed with you. Then maybe, if you still know them or have a way of getting in contact, get in touch and tell them. I bet they'll be delighted.

# 28th March

*"Spring drew on... and a greenness grew over those brown beds, which, freshening daily, suggested the thought that Hope traversed them at night, and left each morning brighter traces of her steps."*
Charlotte Brontë, *Jane Eyre*

Round about now is likely to be the day the clocks change – in Britain at least, where we enter that glorious period: **British Summer Time**. The day when the clocks go back is one of my favourite days! A whole hour of extra light. Think about what you can do with all that daytime! Maybe it means you'll stay up and write or draw late into the evenings. Or does it just mean the beginning of outdoor wine time?

Today, create a story today about someone who finds they have an extra hour. Perhaps it's a magical hour that they can live again – revisiting an hour from their past. Perhaps it is someone who finds they have an extra hour to live – one more hour before the machine is turned off.

Or perhaps it is the simple story of someone who got the time wrong, who decides, against all their normal rush-rush-rush patterns of behaviour to just... stop. And take one hour to just *be*. What does the hour mean to them? And how might it change their life? Feel free to write this or create your story in pictures.

# 29th March

*"Life is a lot like jazz – it's best when you improvise."*
George Gershwin

Today is **World Piano Day**. I want you to pick, at random, a piece of piano music. Perhaps pull out an old vinyl of classical masterpieces and let the needle drop anywhere. Or google 'piano solos' and pick one. Or search on Spotify. However you do it, pick something you don't know well, then sit and listen to it.

And *really* listen. You're going to listen to it three times (at least).

The first time, let it wash over you, take it in, enjoy bathing in it. The second time, you are listening to it for story. Take your pen and make notes. What does the music suggest is happening? Where is it? What landscape does it conjure? What drama? Is it bright and delightful? Romantic? Sombre? Clanging and arrhythmic? Who are these characters?

The third time, you are going to write or draw as you listen, telling the story that has risen out of the music for you. Listen to it as many times as you need. And when you're done and going on with your day, stick this in your creative imagination bank: that it is so easy to put on a piece of music to lift a mood, to reconnect with your imagination, to inspire you. It really is a gift.

# 30th March

*"All creative people should be required
to leave California for three months every year."*
Gloria Swanson

Sometimes it's good to force yourself out of your comfort zone and away from the familiar. For Gloria, that comfort zone is California; for us today, that's our favourite genres.

Come on, be honest – what is the one genre you shy away from, that you'd never write in a million years? Today you're going to write a prose passage or a scene in that genre. And don't cheat! I'm talking about the type of writing that you speed-walk past in the library. (If you still go to libraries. If you don't, you should. Unless they're all closed. In which case, go and protest.)

Here are some genres to choose from. Which one makes you pull away in disgust? It's *that* one! Do it, invest in the tropes of it (if you're not sure, google them) and you never know, you may really enjoy it!

- Romantic comedy
- Murder mystery/whodunnit
- Noir or spy thriller
- Farce
- Horror
- Bashy, crashy military fiction
- Mills and Boon-esque gushy romantic fiction
- Serious olde worlde historical fiction
- Stream-of-consciousness contemporary fiction
- Dystopian fantasy
- Science fiction
- Magic realism

# 31st March

*"Never be afraid to sit a while and think."*
Lorraine Hansberry

It's time for another restrictive writing exercise. Enjoy how the constraints force you to be more creative. Write a passage without once using the letter E. It can't be that hard, I'm sure you're thinking. Let me tell you: it is!

Incredibly, Ernest Vincent Wright managed to sustain it for an entire novel, *Gadsby*, published in 1939, though I wonder if he was disappointed when he realised that the front cover would let him down… seeing as his name was Ernest.

It's your turn to try. It's surprisingly difficult and will, without a doubt, push you to construct your thoughts in a slightly awkward way – as this paragraph shows. I am trying hard to sound natural but it is not as straightforward as you might think!

# April

# 1st April

**April Fools' Day!** Your task is to write a news article about something ridiculous happening, as if it's a fact.

Write with all the conviction of a genuine piece of journalism, channelling the tone of a serious writer. Have a look at well-known examples of the form as inspiration. For example, in 1957 the BBC ran a story about the spaghetti trees that had started popping up all over Switzerland after a pest – 'the spaghetti weevil' – had finally been eradicated. Or in 2016, *National Geographic* ran a story about its decision to no longer print pictures of naked animals.

Choose an event that is an ironic twist on reality, in order to capture the wry wit of a good April Fools' prank.

Best to do this exercise before noon, so you can still fit in a prank or two.

# 2nd April

*"Perhaps when I am famous and my diary is discovered
people will understand the torment of being a 13¾-year-old
undiscovered intellectual."*
Sue Townsend, *The Diary of Adrian Mole, Aged 13¾*

Let's whizz back in time – depending on how old you are. If you're a teenager, lucky you – and plaudits for getting into writing this early. I wish I had.

Think back to a moment in your youth where something dramatic happened. It doesn't have to be a mega drama – you may not have had a life with Shakespearean levels of slings and arrows – any event that was emotional for you will work. A break-up. A first kiss. A lie. A confrontation.

Now, you're going to write about it, as if standing outside yourself, so write either in the third person, or from the perspective of someone else who was there. Think about how to set it up as a story. How you can draw on the details you remember – think of all five senses – and try to plumb them in. This will help you conjure the details for your reader; even the simplest scenario can be captivating on the page if the reader is transported there. Work out what the beginning, middle and end of the drama is, and write those three short parts.

The point is that you're drawing on your own experience but from a new perspective. It can really help your writing if you practise wearing someone else's shoes, and telling a story from a point of view that you wouldn't naturally take. We often want to be the hero. What happens if we're not?

# 3rd April

Today, pick a moment from your own life experience – and then write it as a farcical scene with dialogue. The traits of a farce are wit and comedy, physical comedy ('Who's outside the door?' shenanigans), silliness, mistaken identities, misunderstandings, speed of repartee, and a general brightness. So pick an incident that might lend itself to this and have a go. Put your characters through the wringer... the harder the situation is for them, the funnier it will be.

# 4th April

"You may encounter many defeats, but you must not be defeated. In fact, it may be necessary to encounter the defeats, so you can know who you are, what you can rise from, how you can still come out of it."
Maya Angelou

Today I want you to find a piece of printed writing you can write on. It can be an article in a newspaper or a magazine, or a page of a book you don't mind wrecking (sacrilege!!).

Take a marker pen and start blocking out words you don't find interesting in every line. Linking words are often dull. Repetitive words. Short matter-of-fact words. Or perhaps you love short, sharp words? Perhaps the words that turn you off are the highfalutin, verbose megawords with multiple syllables. Get rid of them! Make sure in every line you only leave a few tip-top words.

You should now have a passage with a scattered collection of excellent words. Make a list of them, putting them in an order that seems delightful to you. What looks pretty going first? Do you want to put all the short words together to create a series of small sounds to enliven your work? Or begin with a gloriously multisyllabic titan of a word as your opener? Do what you like. Go for gold.

Now take a look at your new list. This is your map for today's piece of writing. Write a scene or piece of prose in which you use all the words on your list in your chosen order. Good luck!

# 5th April

*"I don't write every day; it depends on where I am in the project. For the rough draft it's counterproductive if I do it for too long; if I write more than five to six pages a day, my work afterwards is substandard, and it gets confusing if I don't bottle up; the standard has to be kept at a certain level. It's like a jazz musician who gets the best music out and then pulls out. There's always something else productive or administrative to be done."*

Kazuo Ishiguro

Here's today's challenge. Write a dramatic scene with the following elements:

- Two characters.

- One character with an unusual habit.

- The line 'You should have told me. Why didn't you tell me?'

- The knowledge that someone is about to come in.

- A door that can't be locked.

# 6th April

*"Fill your life with diverse and dynamic conversation.
Conversation is the workshop of all good writing."*
Dolly Alderton

Today, you're going to write a conversation in real time as you hear it play out in your head. Don't prepare, just sit quietly and listen. It'll be two people talking. Allow a voice to begin speaking and write down what they say.

Don't give them names. Don't use punctuation. Write freehand. And when the other person answers, write their response on a new line. It might be short. It might be long. It might be mundane. It might be the most important conversation these two people have ever had. Just 'channel it', so to speak, and write down whatever comes into your head without judgement.

Whenever I'm writing drama there comes a point at which the characters 'take over' and converse without me seeming to do much other than listen. I often end up straining to keep pace with the conversation. This is my favourite kind of writing. Of course there's a lot of editing to do down the line, but often the more exciting moments of revelation or surprise in my work happen when I'm not even anticipating it! Frost wasn't wrong when he wisely said, 'No surprise in the writer, no surprise in the reader.' And as for tears – if I'm emotional when I write a scene, it's most often the moment an audience will feel it too.

# 7th April

"While with an eye made quiet by the power
Of harmony, and the deep power of joy,
We see into the life of things."
William Wordsworth, 'Tintern Abbey'

Today is **William Wordsworth's birthday.** The inspired poet was born in 1770 and loved to write about his experience of nature and the world around him. He famously used to set out on foot at any hour of the day, often early morning or late at night, to find inspiration. He even hopped over to France for a walking tour in his twenties, as a way to get his creative thoughts whirring.

So, in honour of good old Will, today you're going to take a walk in the most beautiful place you can. Don't just go round the block. Make a journey to steep yourself in 'proper' nature. If you possibly can, city-dwellers, get out of town and into an expanse of green. Or go to the seaside. Why not? There is something about being able to see a horizon that is mind-clearing; and, moreover, allows you to actually *think* in a different way – when your eyes stop focusing on something close by, your facial muscles relax, which in turn shifts your focus. True fact!

Go and walk and take in everything you see. Try to imagine how a nature poet would see what you're seeing. What would they notice? What would inspire them? Write it down, or draw it, then find somewhere to park yourself and write. It could be a poem, it could be prose, the intention is to appreciate what you see and experience today. Thanks, Wordsworth!

APRIL

# 8th April

*"I wish I were one of those people who wrote songs quickly.
But I'm not. So it takes me a great deal of time to find out
what the song is."*
Leonard Cohen

Today, write out the alphabet from A to Z. You are going to make up a new verb for each letter of the alphabet. You might like to create new words using sounds that you find entertaining. To 'biffle', for example, might be to sneeze very quietly. Or to 'choop' might mean to lope along: 'He chooped past, trousers hanging low, giving me the side-eye.'

Or, you can use bits of words you know and stick them together to work out a new word hybrid. To 'franzijig', for example, a hybrid of 'frantic' and 'jig', might mean to dance wildly: 'I've neven seen anyone franzijig like that!' Or to 'archiwaffle' might mean to bore your peers with made-up historical facts in order to impress them: '"You know that old wall was actually the very wall that Harold VII hid his armies behind during the second war of the Roses," he archiwaffled, as she smiled politely, whilst mentally noting *never* to agree to a blind date again.'

Write out your new made-up words – and an example for each of how you'd use it in a sentence. Get creative!

# 9th April

*"The music is not in the notes, but in the silence between."*
Wolfgang Amadeus Mozart

So here's some science for you. It's been analysed and proven that listening to Mozart increases your level of focus. That's because his music specifically affects your 'spatial-temporal reasoning'; in other words, your concentration, which is why so many revision programmes and schools encourage their students to listen to his music while they work.

Here's today's task. You are going to write a piece with one of the following four titles, each inspired by a work of his. It doesn't have to be anything to do with Mozart – though if you want to set your scene in a pretty Austrian piazza in the mid-eighteenth century then be my guest. And as you write, listen to Mozart. Any Mozart you like, but Mozart. And see how his music helps you get into your writing groove.

Here are your titles to choose from:

- *The Magic Flute*
- *Queen of the Night*
- *The Marriage of Figaro*
- *Coronation Mass*

# 10th April

*"Create people, not types."*
F. Scott Fitzgerald

All too often, when discussing writing, someone will ask: 'What sort of person is this character?' And I never know what to say, because what they are after is some sort of definable, singular character trait. They want to know whether the character is an angry person? Or shy? Or happy? Beware! No real people are definable by a single trait.

Think about all the people you know. Could you describe any of them as an 'anything' sort of person? I couldn't. The brightest optimists have days of absolute misery. The quieter ones are occasionally the loudest person in the room. People are a glorious mess of contradictions. They are reluctant enthusiasts, envious givers, cheerful pessimists. And it's these clashing traits that make people interesting. And *real*.

As that sage F. Scott Fitzgerald advised in his 'Seven Tips for Writing': *'Begin with an individual, and before you know it you find that you have created a type; begin with a type, and you find that you have created – nothing.'*

Today's exercise is simple. Make four lists: outwardly positive qualities (generous, cheery, loving, bright); negative qualities (sad, angry, covetous, malicious); age groups (primary-schooler, emo teens, mid-life crisis-er); and professions (flower arranger, cleaner, shoplifter). Cut the lists up and pick, at random, one choice from each category. This is your character description. What did you pick? Maybe an honest but cruel, middle-aged butcher. Or a kind but gossipy, teenage Ultimate Frisbee player.

Make a few options then pick your favourite. Handy hint: the more unlikely the combination, the more interesting. I'd much rather write about a shoplifting granny than a shoplifting teen.

Write one paragraph in their voice, and if you like them, write more!

# 11th April

*"For our vanity is such that we hold our own characters immutable, and we are slow to acknowledge that they have changed, even for the better."*
E. M. Forster

It's true, I think, that a deep understanding of your own psychology helps you to write other people well. We need to remain interested in and alert to what makes us tick, what motivates us, how our present-day predilections and personality have been formed through experience.

Today's task is to answer the following questions about *yourself*. In detail. Some may seem simplistic, but I promise you, the simpler they appear, the more complex the answers can be. Take time thinking about each question – and try to be as honest as possible. It's easy to deny those truths we don't like very much, but trust me, it's worth it. If you can do this analysis for yourself, you can do it for any character you'll ever write.

Here are the Ten Self-Analysis Questions:

1. Who are you?

2. If you had to define yourself in a single word, what would it be?

3. What do you like most about yourself?

4. If you could change something about yourself: a) what would it be and b) would you do it? (It's not reversible!)

5. What is the secret you've never told anyone?

6. What are you most ashamed of?

7. To whom do you owe the most and why?

8. Who do you think loves you the most – and why do they? What is it that they love about you?

9. What trait of yours are you most proud of, and do you hope other people recognise?

10. If there's one thing – and one thing only – you could wish for your future, what would it be?

# 12th April

*"As a writer, one is allowed to have conversations with oneself. What is considered sane in writers is mad for the rest of the human race."*
Alan Ayckbourn

Happy birthday, **Alan Ayckbourn**. Oh, Alan, how do you do it? Ayckbourn is *prolific*. Most folks would proud of finishing one play in a lifetime. Alan writes one every year, minimum So, inspired by his capacity to create, here we go.

Your task today is to pick one of the following titles, all Ayckbourn plays, as your writing prompt, and write a scene based on it. If you know the play, don't pick that one; the title is meant as a blank-canvas starting point... I want you to respond to the words alone, not to any preconception of what you think Ayckbourn's version might be.

- *Snake in the Grass*

- *Way Upstream*

- *Miss Yesterday*

- *Neighbourhood Watch*

- *Bedroom Farce*

# 13th April

*"Ever tried. Ever failed. No matter.*
*Try again. Fail again. Fail better."*
Samuel Beckett

Today is two great days: it's **Samuel Beckett's birthday** *and* it's **National Scrabble Day**. Double whammy! So today we're going to play a party game... using Scrabble.

Ideally, you will use a Scrabble set, so if you have one, put out all the tiles upside down, then group them into piles of seven letters. When I say go, you're going to make a word out of each pile. It doesn't need to use all seven letters, but you only get one word per pile. Make words you think are interesting, amusing or dramatic. Ready... GO!

If you don't have a Scrabble set, sad times. Cut up the alphabet three times over to make yourself a good letter selection – ta-dah, DIY Scrabble!

When you have your list of words, put them in an exciting order. This is the framework for your story. Make a plan for what each word inspires in the action – is it a character, an event, a location? Now create your story, either in words or pictures.

# 14th April

*"If you want to be good at anything, you have to work hard at it. It doesn't just fall from the sky. I work every day at trying to improve my writing, and I really enjoy it.*
*Nothing fascinates me more than putting words together, and seeing how a collection of words can produce quite a profound effect."*
PJ Harvey

PJ Harvey is very wise, and enormously creative. But on this day – which is officially **Look Up at the Sky Day** – I'm actually going to counter her suggestion that ideas don't just fall from the sky... because that's exactly where we are going to source our starting point.

Go and lie down outside, or sit by a window if it's too cold. I'd recommend lying down in the fresh air, as you'll find it much easier to throw yourself into this imaginatively.

I want you to watch the sky. Watch it for at least five minutes. Watch it change. And watch the clouds. What can you see? What shapes do they make? Which characters arise? Take note of everything that might feed into a story. Perhaps it's a feeling you get from looking at the vastness above you. Perhaps the clouds are skittish and playful. Perhaps you can see a giant hot dog, or a swirling monster. Perhaps there isn't a single cloud and a feeling of peace descends. Perhaps there's an ominous storm brewing. Now spend a second five minutes, still looking up, but now mentally putting together an outline for a story or scene.

And then guess what: go and write it!

# 15th April

*"No longer shall I paint interiors with men reading and women knitting. I will paint living people who breathe and feel and suffer and love."*
Edvard Munch

It's **World Art Day**! What a great day. Today I want you to find two different paintings, by two different artists that you find inspiring. They should be scenes featuring people.

Your task is to mash the ideas together from these two source pieces and create a scenario. Perhaps the characters from each painting literally meet one another. Perhaps the sense of mystery in one might help develop a story of the other. Perhaps Hockney's swimming pool might be the setting where Munch's screaming figure confronts the reason for their anxiety.

Enjoy the eccentricities and odd juxtaposition that happen when you throw together two contrasting sources, and rather than battling against them, embrace them instead.

# 16th April

"Song-writing is like a thunderstorm building up inside me.
If I don't write songs, I get all bottled up. It's almost like
a survival mechanism. For me, music has to have a little
speck of intrigue or the unknown. Also, I'm an old-school
romantic in the sense that even if you write songs about dark
stuff, the root of the song should be about going through the
tunnel and coming out on the other side with a happy ending.
I'm not into songs that are just about self-pity or self-
indulgence. I usually look at songs as little trips that show you
going on your way to some other place."

Björk

Inspired by Björk (who isn't?!), your task today is to write a journey piece – where someone goes through a trial and comes out the other side. It could be a literal journey: someone gets stuck in a tunnel. It could be an emotional challenge: the first journey out after a long spell in prison. It could be an internal journey. Up to you.

Write it as a passage in the third person, viewing our protagonist and their experience from the outside.

Or, if you *really* want to be like Björk, you can write it as a song.

# 17th April

*"An opening line should invite the reader to begin the story.
It should say: Listen. Come in here.
You want to know about this…"*
Stephen King

It's a tough ask – but an important one. After all, you only have one opening line in each piece of writing! You also only get one ending line. And that's the line that'll stick with a reader while they sit and digest what they've read, so that too is an incredibly important sentence.

Your task today is to come up with ten brilliant opening lines, and ten brilliant closing lines for a novel. That's it! See how far you can draw your readers in within the constraints of a single sentence.

# 18th April

*"Journalism makes you think fast. You have to speak to people in all walks of life."*
Terry Pratchett

It's **National Columnists' Day,** so today's task requires you to whip out your best journalistic skills. You're going to write an interview, imagining both the interviewer and the interviewee.

Pick someone characterful to write about. It could be someone real and fascinating, or you can make someone up. Then choose who is going to interview them. Give your fictional journalist a specific tone and agenda to add spice to the scenario. Write the interview in the style of an editorial piece, whether it's a think piece for a Sunday broadsheet or a glossy gossip rag.

Make sure that the reader gets a sense of the interviewer's personality as much as the interviewee by choosing this vocabulary and syntax specifically. Read a few examples online or in print to give you some inspiration. It's amazing how much we learn about the interviewer from their attitudes and the questions they choose to ask... often as much as the interviewee!

# 19th April

"For my own part, if a book is well written,
I always find it too short."
Jane Austen

Your task today is to write a review of a story you've read or seen recently. It could be a novel, a television show, a film, a play. It's a useful tool, as a writer, to be able to analyse why a story works for you.

Write about the narrative specifically – we're not looking in this instance about how good an actor's performance was, for example, or how much you lusted over the costumes. Think about what worked about the story, what didn't, and what you might have suggested to the writer if you were advising them, like an editor or a dramaturg. When you're done, see if you can make a list of these elements or qualities, as a guide – if you will – for good storytelling. Then come back and re-read your list when you're writing your own work.

# 20th April

*"All my books are about one major idea and two or three subsidiary ones. I have thought a lot about music when constructing books, and I like the way in music that themes come back."*
Sebastian Faulks

Happy birthday, **Sebastian Faulks**. In his honour, today's tip is inspired by his quote above which, if you've read any of his novels, will make a lot of sense – his writing is beautifully structured and always poetic.

Today your task is to write a short story or scene inspired by one of the following musical forms. Pick one, listen to some examples, think about what world they conjure up for you, then have a go!

- Country music

- A sonata

- Ragtime

- Folk ballads

- Operetta

- Brass band

- Classical piano

- Electronic music

# 21st April

*"When authors write best, or, at least, when they write most fluently, an influence seems to waken in them which becomes their master – which will have its way – putting out of view all behests but its own, dictating certain words, and insisting on their being used, whether vehement or measured in their nature, new moulding characters, giving unthought of turns to incidents, rejecting carefully elaborated old ideas, and suddenly creating and adopting new ones."*
Charlotte Brontë

Charlotte Brontë is probably best known as the author of *Jane Eyre*. It's a story of a young girl's struggles against the hard circumstances that she's thrown into. It includes – famously – Mrs Rochester, the 'mad wife', whom Rochester has hidden from society and locked in a room on the third floor... until Jane discovers her.

Today's task is to write a story about a character hidden in a room. Perhaps it's from the perspective of the person hidden, perhaps the person hiding them, perhaps the person who finds them. Are they locked in or do they choose to be there? Are they hiding from the world or desperate to engage with it? Is it for specific reasons? Are they trapped? And what's the consequence, psychologically, of staying in one room for years?

If you need inspiration for a different version of this story, try googling 'medieval anchoresses' and 'Julian of Norwich'. Both fascinating and terrifying!

# 22nd April

*"I find I write best when I sit myself down, have a coffee, go into wherever my space is, and I have to have something that I like to look at because there's a lot of dead time in the writing process... I like to have a view of the ocean."*
Billy Joel

Time for more writer training.

We're going to do a HIIT class – short, sharp exercises to get your brain and vocab in gear. Do these to get your writing muscles activated.

Set a timer and do each of the following for *two minutes* each, as many as you can in the time:

1. Write a list of words to do with the sea.

2. Write a list of adjectives (descriptive words) beginning with 'C'.

3. Write a list of verbs (doing words) beginning with 'R'.

4. Write a list of words that make you feel calm.

5. Write a list of all the words you can think of that include the word 'ate'.

6. Write a list of invented names for weird, hitherto undiscovered deep-sea creatures.

APRIL

# 23rd April

*"My mistress' eyes are nothing like the sun;*
*Coral is far more red than her lips' red;*
*If snow be white, why then her breasts are dun;*
*If hairs be wires, black wires grow on her head.*
*I have seen roses damasked, red and white,*
*But no such roses see I in her cheeks;*
*And in some perfumes is there more delight*
*Than in the breath that from my mistress reeks.*
*I love to hear her speak, yet well I know*
*That music hath a far more pleasing sound;*
*I grant I never saw a goddess go;*
*My mistress, when she walks, treads on the ground.*
*And yet, by heaven, I think my love as rare*
*As any she belied with false compare."*
William Shakespeare, Sonnet 130

Today is **Shakespeare's birthday** – *and* **National 'Talk Like Shakespeare' Day**. So today – in his honour – we're going to write a sonnet.

A sonnet has fourteen lines and is usually written in iambic pentameter (five pairs of weak-strong syllables: de DUH de DUH de DUH de DUH de DUH). Shakespearean sonnets are usually made up of four parts, three quatrains (rhyming ABAB, CDCD, EFEF,) then a final couplet (GG) that answers or twists the sentiment to give a little surprise at the end of the poem.

My favourite of all Shakespeare's sonnets is Sonnet 130 (yep, he wrote a lot). It talks about how lacking in conventional beauty the 'mistress' is. It seems like the opposite of a love poem, but then, in a brilliant lyrical twist, he turns that round at the end, and uses the last couplet to prove how deep his love is for this earthly mistress. In writing your own sonnet see if you can get a good twist in the last two lines – it's *very* satisfying.

# 24th April

*"Forgive your enemies. But never forget their names."*
John F. Kennedy

Today we're going to think about names. Naming characters can be one of the most fun parts of writing. I often change the name of key characters midway through, as I realise my initial choice somehow doesn't *feel* right in my bones. You know when it's right – that person 'pops'. They make sense and they suit their name. So here's a simple way to begin thinking about people who might crop up in your stories.

Write down a list of twenty first names. Think of unusual ones. You can always cast your eye towards a bookshelf or into a magazine (hint: the more specific the magazine, the better… There are some brilliant names in posh magazines like *Town and Country* and *The Lady*, or some excellent choices in magazines about wicca or horoscopes).

Then write down a list of twenty surnames. Some of these should be chosen for their sound. Do they have long, languid sounds – like Madame Mourunier, for example, or Mr Dougherty – or short pops – a Mr Nib, for example, or Ms Blick? Are the names overly fussy or image-conjuring? Do they speak to someone's profession, or give us a hint where they're from?

Now have a go at pairing these up. Give your twenty characters second names from the list. Some will be an obvious pair. Others you might choose because they're an odd juxtaposition.

And there you go: a cast of characters! Choose a couple, decide where and when they are from, jot down some details about their lives and draw a picture of them. And if you feel inspired, then write something in their voice.

# 25th April

*"If you were going to die soon and had only one phone call you could make, who would you call and what would you say? And why are you waiting?"*
Stephen Levine

Mr Levine asks us a very good question. On this, **International Telephone Day,** you are going to write, as a monologue, a voicemail message: the message that someone leaves as their last call on Earth.

What are the circumstances? Where are they going? Why it is their last call? Think what might be fun to write. This doesn't have to be the sombre 'dying' call – though it could be – but it could also be someone leaving to go off-grid, take flight to another planet with no chance of return, or an act-of-vengeance call telling their children/ partner/mother/enemy exactly what they think of them – and how they're going to punish them for the rift they caused… maybe by leaving their fortune to the donkey sanctuary, rather than to their ungrateful kids.

Enjoy the drama of being able to write a one-sided conversation. It means your character can speak from their heart, knowing full well that there'll be no comeback.

# 26th April

*"The earth has its music for those who will listen."*
Reginald Vincent Holmes

Today, inspired by nature, you're going to imagine a countryside landscape. It could be the vista from an Umbrian hill, looking over the cypress tree-peppered meadows. The view from Machu Picchu over the Peruvian rainforests. A view of the churning ocean from a Scottish island. Take yourself anywhere in the world.

Now, imagine you're looking at this view some time in distant history – perhaps medieval times, perhaps even more ancient than that, or perhaps the turn of the twentieth century. Choose a character – the person looking at the view – and write a scene detailing what they are watching. Who, in this period, interests you? Think about the action that they can see. Are they watching events playing out? Or simply observing a quiet countryside day? Step into their shoes, considering not only what they can see, but how they *feel* about it.

When you've completed this, skip forward, leaping through time to another era. Pick a decade from the twentieth or twenty-first century – perhaps a moment in the Roaring Twenties, or the Swinging Sixties, or today. Choose a new character standing in the same spot and repeat the exercise, considering what now plays out on your landscape. What's the same and what has changed?

Finally, repeat the exercise, choosing a moment in the future. Perhaps it's just a few years hence, or perhaps it's a huge leap in to the distant future. Choose another character and do the exercise one last time. Then, when you're done, have a read back and consider how the landscape these characters find themselves in might allow us to see connections between people with otherwise completely different lives.

# 27th April

*"It's very helpful to start with something that's true. If you start with something that's false, you're always covering your tracks. Something simple and true, that has a lot of possibilities, is a nice way to begin."*
Paul Simon

Today is a simple writing-prompt day.

Think of something personal to you. It could be a worry you have. A secret you keep. A memory you cherish. A quandary you're in. Anything – as long as you are prepared to write about it authentically, from the heart with no denial.

Set your timer for ten minutes and free-write. And if, at the end of the ten minutes, if you feel like carrying on, be my guest!

# 28th April

*"For an author, the nice characters aren't much fun.
What you want are the screwed-up characters.
You know, the characters that are constantly wondering if
what they are doing is the right thing, characters that are not
only screwed-up but are self-tapping screws.
They're doing it for themselves."*
Terry Pratchett

It's the wonderful, much-missed **Terry Pratchett's birthday** today. And he's right: fun characters to write are full of flaws, foibles, oddities; the underdogs, not the great successes. Today, you're going to write the opening paragraphs of a novel starring a loser. Someone who is unfortunate, or unpopular, perhaps antisocial, perhaps the runt of the litter.

This person is *not* a winner – and that's exactly why we will love them. Because they have a journey to go on. Write these first paragraphs in the protagonist's voice, choosing carefully how they speak – their syntax, vocabulary, specifics of accent or dialect, age, class.

The protagonist is going to talk to the audience and introduce their story, revealing why they are (or were) a loser, and setting up the fact that that all might change. Try to capture a feeling of excitement about the story to come. Where has this character got to go, and how can you hint at that to draw your readers in?

# 29th April

*"With enough courage, you can do without a reputation."*
Margaret Mitchell

Today, you can write what you like – the only rule is that you're going to write it standing or lying down. See what happens to your ideas when you have the weirdness of writing in a position you don't usually write in. Does it make you write quickly? Does it change the tone? What, imaginatively, does this alternative process kick-start? You'll be in good company: apparently Ernest Hemingway wrote all his novels standing up and Truman Capote wrote all his lying down.

And if you need a specific idea of what to write, how about a three-way dialogue between people in a room, one sitting, one standing and one lying down?

APRIL

# 30th April

*"Just don't give up trying to do what you really want to do.
Where there is love and inspiration,
I don't think you can go wrong."*
Ella Fitzgerald

It's **National Jazz Day**, so let's celebrate the brilliance of the form – by improvising and scat writing! Scat singing is improvised words, sung to a jazz melody, using a mixture of nonsense sounds ('ba-dee ba-doo bah', for example), onomatopoeia and sounds that mimic instruments making music ('Schweeeeee! Darrrumm darrrum darrrum').

Your task is to improvise a story song, using this as your mode of writing. Enjoy the freedom of the form – and by all means, make it up by singing it if you fancy! Try to write a song if you can, using a mixture of real words and improvised 'scat' words. You'll find the permission to use sounds and non-words will free you up immensely and bring a sense of playfulness to your process.

And if you need inspiration, treat your ears to Ella Fitzgerald singing, 'How High the Moon', the 1966 recording. Truly epic.

# May

# 1st May

*"There's a starman waiting in the sky,*
*He'd like to come and meet us,*
*But he thinks he'd blow our minds..."*
David Bowie, 'Starman'

David Bowie wrote extraordinary songs. His poetic lyrics are constantly surprising – sometimes narrative, sometimes riffing on a theme, sometimes they're just plain odd – but they are never boring.

One of his best-loved songs is 'Starman' (and guess what? The first Friday in May is appropriately **Space Day**). In it, he imagines that a 'starman' from space is communicating with us, sharing a bright and love-filled message for humans. Have a listen. It's a gorgeous song. And while you do, find some pieces of writing – either pieces of a newspaper, a magazine, a page of your notebook, a poem you like, and cut them up into bits. Each 'bit' may have no more than a few words on it. Now spread these all out and reorder them. And make a new piece. This is your cut-up.

Bowie used 'cut-ups' a lot to form his songs. He described their magic creative potential as a 'very Western Tarot' as it yields all sorts of things you could never have predicted:

> *'What I've used it for... is igniting anything that might be in my imagination... I tried doing it with diaries and things, and I was finding out amazing things about me and what I'd done and where I was going.'*

As a Brixton resident, I have a huge soft spot for Bowie. He lived in my little corner of London and you can still feel his magic here. I hope you enjoy this method as much as he did. If nothing else, whack on a Bowie record, lie back and enjoy – maybe that's enough for today. It's certainly inspiration.

MAY

# 2nd May

Today is **National Scrapbook Day**... or very close to it (it's the first Saturday in May).

So for today's task I'd like you to find a magazine or a newspaper, and look for related images that catch your eye. Choose a theme inspired by this content. Perhaps they are all political in some way, featuring representation or body image. Perhaps it's a colour or a texture that makes you *feel* something. Perhaps it's a tone: comic, mysterious, gossipy. Or a subject such as women playing sport or cute dogs or crazy accidents, depending on which magazine you're looking at.

Assemble a bunch of images. Stick them onto a large piece of paper and then look for the story. Inspired by what you see, write either a monologue or the opening of a story with these ideas as your jumping-off point, or create a visual story – or a comic-strip storyboard, for example, to tell today's tale.

MAY

# 3rd May

*"The most common way people give up their power
is by thinking they don't have any."*
Alice Walker

Today, on **World Press Freedom Day**, your task is to write a speech about power. You can take that instruction in any way you want. It can be a call-to-arms, addressing thousands at a rally, a union, a meeting or an election stump (a politician's speech made when running for office). It could be a personal story, addressing a handful. Or a speech to a council, asking for a law change, a prisoner addressing a court to plead for their freedom, or a politician announcing a new policy… it's up to you!

Think about the qualities that make a powerful speech. Here are a few tips to think about:

- Make sure it has a clear structure, so it is direct and to the point.

- Use facts (if relevant). Make sure they're carefully researched. You can use specific examples, numbers or details to reinforce your cause.

- A sense of writing for your specific audience, to capture their hearts. How old are they? How formal is the setting? Write accordingly.

- Use rhetorical language to draw them in.

- Be concise. Make sure you don't lose the focus and aim to keep it short.

- Be clear and defined, so your speech is unambiguous and your message is clear.

- And be interesting! There's no point in making a speech if you don't entertain the audience, as they won't listen to a word of it!

# 4th May

*"Spring is the time of plans and projects."*
Leo Tolstoy

Weather plays such a crucial role in the tonal setting for so many stories. A storm, a heatwave or endless rains are often a sign of something disturbed in the heart of the novel's protagonists or their community. Today is **National Weather Observers' Day** and so you're going to write in detail about a weather event, and one person at the centre of that. But here's the challenge: let's do the *opposite* of what we might usually do in a task like this.

Write your character having a counter-reaction to the rest of the population. Someone in the middle of torrential rain is delighting in it. Someone out on the roof as the storm descends decides to gleefully drink in the thunder. Someone in the dust bowl of the heatwave couldn't be happier to step out onto the red-hot earth. Enjoy writing their reaction, and the reason for it, and juxtapose that with the rest of the community. How do the two interact?

MAY

# 5th May

"At first I had no skills in writing comedy.
I didn't know what a joke was, but, as someone once told me,
your emotions follow your intent. If you create the intention
of starting a comedy act, slowly your mind starts adjusting
and you arrive at a new emotional state."
Steve Martin

Today is a simple writing-prompt day. Your task is to write about:

*What happened to the woman when she discovered who her parents really were?*

But – because around this date (the first Sunday in May) is **World Laughter Day** – it has to be *funny*. Who are the most unlikely parents? Or *what* are they?

You can write it either as prose or dialogue… or try both… and see which you find it easier to 'find the funny' in.

# 6th May

Set a timer for ten minutes. I want you to free-write a piece of fiction until the timer goes. If you stop for a moment, write the word 'rubbish' repeatedly until you get your flow back. And the first line of your free-write is: *'When the doors didn't open...'*

Try your best to complete a story by the time the timer goes. If you want to set an interim alarm at seven minutes to tell you that you should be heading for the ending, do.

When you've done this, you're going to do a hard edit of the work. Cut everything you don't like. Rewrite. Reorder. Reshape. Rethink. But work with focus until the buzzer goes.

Then go for a walk around the room/garden/block, wherever you happen to be. Go away from your work for at least ten minutes (but no more than twenty – we're still working, slacker).

Now return to it, and do another edit. You might be amazed how much easier this is, having not looked at it for a bit.

Repeat these last two steps until you're happy with it.

MAY

# 7th May

*"There are some words that once spoken will split the world in two. There would be the life before you breathed them and then the altered life after they'd been said. They take a long time to find words like that. They make you hesitate. Choose with care."*
Andrea Levy

Which are the best books you've ever read? Some books stay with us because the writing is extraordinary. Others because something in a protagonist chimes with our hearts at that specific point in our lives. Perhaps it's a tone that you particularly enjoyed; perhaps a book brought you escapism at a tough moment. Perhaps you met a heroine you aspire to be more like. Whatever the reason, your task today is to write a list of your favourite books, and one (only one!) line about each, which encapsulates why it's on the list. The list can be as long as you like. You can include books you remember from childhood. Any stories that have enriched your life.

When you're done, look at the list, try to identify any themes or overarching trends. What do these books say about you… and might this help you realise what *you* want to write?

# 8th May

*"If you are a writer you're at home, which means you're out of touch. You have to make excuses to get out there and look at how the world is changing."*
Roddy Doyle

Today we're going to piggy-back on yesterday's task and use it as a starting point. Yesterday, I asked you to make a list of your favourite books and work out if there were any themes or trends.

I now want you to write a single line – a title, if you will – that encapsulates the theme of your list. It could be a question: 'What does it mean to love?'; or a concept that many of the books have in common: 'Underdog comes of age'; it could be a notion: 'Improving the world in small acts'; or a tone or genre like 'magical realism'. Make this idea a sentence that sounds like a good title. Then write the opening pages of a novel with that title.

Who knows, maybe your book will make in onto someone else's favourites list one day!

# 9th May

*"I write plays about things that I can't resolve in my mind.
I try to root things out."*
Alan Bennett

One of Bennett's best-loved works is his *Talking Heads* TV series – character monologues by quirky individuals, often rather everyday people with everyday experiences but who are so carefully drawn that we thoroughly enjoy watching them. It is the minutiae of their lives, foibles and experiences that we identify with and find amusing.

So today – **Alan Bennett's birthday** – I'd like you to think of a problem that, as he suggests, your character can't resolve. A great-grandma trying to work out how to use WhatsApp. A tourist trying to find a friend in a big city. A woman not being able to comprehend why her fertility treatment has failed. The person's problem is the heart of your monologue.

Now write using direct address – i.e. your character talks directly to the audience about their dilemma. Give it shape – try to find an engaging beginning, middle and end. Think carefully about how they might speak: accent, local dialect, class, their range of vocabulary, how formal or informal, how they think, what they choose *not* to say. Where they are when they are speaking to their audience. Are they wholly focused or might they be distracted by what's going on around them? Is there a naughty dog that they tell off, interrupting their delivery, or are they offering the listener tea?

When you're finished, consider writing a second monologue for a character who has a relationship with the first and their dilemma. Is it a member of the council, who has received endless complaints from your original speaker? Is it the infertile woman's partner, not knowing how to help his girlfriend? How can this second scene give us a fuller sense of story?

# 10th May

*"Creativity is a gift. It doesn't come through
if the air is cluttered."*
John Lennon

Write an advert for a book you're going to write. It begins, 'Coming soon, an astonishing new novel by [...], in which [...]'

There you go. In which... what? Use this opportunity to write a thrilling premise. What would you be excited to read? And via that, work out what you will be excited to write. Write this blurb for the cover as if it's a finished book and see what comes out if you just free-write it. Then edit it to really get your head around what you might genuinely like to write.

The great thing about a blurb is that you leave the audience wanting more, the questions are open-ended... you don't need to solve them yet, wait till you write the book! But the hope is that, by writing the premise, you get thinking and start to focus your ideas towards a story you genuinely would like to dive into.

# 11th May

Time for some quick-fire imaginative writing, inspired by my dad's favourite musician, Jimi Hendrix. His lyrics were always imaginative and lifted the listener from their everyday life into a different place or experience.

Today, choose a musician – Jimi is good one, but there's a plethora of choices. Ideally pick someone with interesting lyrics that tell stories. Good choices might be artists like Nick Drake, Tracy Chapman, Elton John, Paul Simon, Eminem, Joni Mitchell, Leonard Cohen, Little Simz, Lizzo or Kendrick Lamar.

Now, pick five of their songs and write out the first line of each. Use each of the five opening lines as a paragraph prompt, i.e. write the rest of the paragraph for each of the starter lines. Write in the voice of the speaker (the singer), so your prose is in the first person. Try not to use your knowledge of the rest of the song to influence what you write… the prompt is merely the first line of the song. Everything that happens after that is up to you!

MAY

# 12th May

*"The Owl and the Pussy-Cat went to sea*
*In a beautiful pea-green boat,*
*They took some honey, and plenty of money,*
*Wrapped up in a five-pound note.*
*The Owl looked up to the stars above,*
*And sang to a small guitar,*
*'O lovely Pussy! O Pussy, my love,*
*What a beautiful Pussy you are,*
*You are,*
*You are!*
*What a beautiful Pussy you are!'"*

Edward Lear

**Edward Lear**, born on this day, was a fabulous writer of strange and inventive tales. For today's task, we'll use his classic poem 'The Owl and the Pussy-cat', and ask what happens next. The stage is set. A little boat bobbing, our two protagonists on board, weighed down with honey… pause there.

Honey? Why? Neither owls nor cats eat honey, do they? Was it back-up medicine in case either needed a natural treatment for a wound? Or were they planning to tempt some wasps to join the party? And the money? Where exactly are they going to spend it?

Our Owl is clearly on a seduction mission, but is it working? Is our cat into him or is this a blind date that she's rapidly regretting?

I am, of course, assuming that Pussy-Cat is the lady in this equation, though there's no evidence. Perhaps it's the other way round. Or perhaps they're both women, or men, or non-binary…

Whatever is going on, I want you to write the rest of the dialogue. What does Cat say when Owl tells them they're beautiful? And how does Cat feel about being called Pussy? I know what I'd say to that, and it would *not* be polite…

# 13th May

*"Writers should be read, but neither seen nor heard."*
Daphne du Maurier

It's **Daphne du Maurier's birthday**, and to celebrate, we're going to take some ingredients from her work and make something new.

Your task is to write a scene for a dark mystery. If you want some ideas, take a look at her work – she was a master of the genre. Although she was classed as a romantic novelist, most of her books delve into something spooky and even paranormal, with a pulsing vein of suspense running through them.

Here are your scene ingredients:

- Pick two protagonists from this list, each name being the title of a du Maurier book: Rebecca, Mary Ann, The Doll, My Cousin Rachel, Julius.

- Pick a setting for your scene from the following, also titles of her stories: Jamaica Inn, The House on the Strand, Castle Dor or Hungry Hill.

- Now pick a title for your scene from one of hers: *The Glass-blowers, The Parasites, The Scapegoat, The Birds.*

Go!

# 14th May

*"So long as you write what you wish to write, that is all that matters; and whether it matters for ages or only for hours, nobody can say."*
Virginia Woolf

Let's take Virginia's words literally. Today, set your timer for twenty minutes and write anything you want to write. Absolutely anything. And enjoy the freedom.

# 15th May

*"I have a feeling we're not in Kansas any more."*
Dorothy Gale in *The Wizard of Oz*

Today we're going to write a scenario inspired by Oz, as it's the birthday of **L. Frank Baum**, creator of *The Wizard of Oz*.

Write a two-hander scene in which a character wakes up to find they are somewhere completely unexpected, as Dorothy does in *The Wizard of Oz*. What happened? How did they get here? Are they waking up in a new universe? In a hospital bed after an accident? Having been reborn? After a big night with someone unexpected in the bed next to them?

Whichever alternative to Kansas you pick, choose something juicy. Your second character – whom your character meets in this new place – must be from this place and therefore familiar with it. They are your tool to allow your protagonist to understand where they are.

MAY

163

# 16th May

*"I was aware that the teaching of drawing was being stopped almost thirty years ago. And I always said, 'The teaching of drawing is the teaching of looking.' A lot of people don't look very hard."*
David Hockney

On **National Drawing Day**, I want you to draw someone. Perhaps straight out of your imagination. Perhaps go to the window and draw a passer-by. Or draw a character you've been working on for a while. How does the act of finding a physical rendering of the person help you to work out their character?

Try drawing several sketches of your character in different scenarios. This will require you to consider their physicality in contrasting states, perhaps emotionally as well as physically.

Choose scenarios which throw your character into different emotional states. One may be super-relaxed in the bath. One when they accidentally electrocute themselves. One where they receive shocking news.

Pick a scenario you enjoyed sketching and write a passage based on it. It could be in the first or third person, but try to encompass what you've learnt about your protagonist from drawing them into the way you write them.

# 17th May

*"Until you're ready to look foolish,
you'll never have the possibility of being great."*
Cher

When you're writing a musical, you're often reminded that characters should sing what they can't say – they are more truthful in sung lyrics than they are in spoken dialogue. This partly explains why pop music often endures in the palpitating hearts of young people, because the singers (often as a character) sing with a depth of emotion that most of us find difficult to express in conversation.

So today, go to your music collection and pick a song with an interesting narrative voice. Jot down some notes on who the narrator is. Are they spurned in love, blaming their lover for giving love a bad name? Are they perving on the schoolteacher, which is what they go to school for? Are they feeling anxious about getting to the office and working 9 to 5?

Now pick a second song and repeat the process. Pick a different genre of music for interest. Note down everything you imagine about this person: who, why, what's their backstory, what are they doing, do we like them, what might they look like?

You now have two characters. And a story for each of them. What happens when they meet? Write a scene in which you smash these two characters and their stories together and see what happens. Is one of them the subject of the other's song? It could be a *very* interesting story cocktail!

# 18th May

*"With every single book, you're sent back to 'Go', and you can strive your little heart out. I think, if anything, writing books gets harder and if it's not getting harder, you're not paying attention and you're starting to manufacture the same thing over and over again. It becomes more and more challenging and that rescues me from any self-satisfaction and stasis."*
Lionel Shriver

Today is **Lionel Shriver's birthday.** To celebrate her notion that you have to start again each time, that we must never be static as writers, today you are going to set a timer for eight minutes and write as many first sentences of a story as you can think of. Try to vary them in tone and style. Let your imagination go wild. A beginning is always a possibility...

MAY

# 19th May

*"I try to write parts for women that are as complicated and interesting as women actually are."*
Nora Ephron

Today is birthday of one of my heroes, screenwriter extraordinaire, and master (mistress) of the romcom, **Nora Ephron**.

Cooking up a great romcom requires several specific ingredients, one of which is a well-chosen pair of lovers to pit against each other. Whilst some rely on two 'meant to be' souls meeting each other, many of the best rely on our two opposites – lovers for whom the other represents everything they *wouldn't* want in a partner.

Take a look at Nora's back catalogue for some examples. In *You've Got Mail*, a small-time independent bookshop owner, passionately averse to big business, falls (unbeknownst to her) for the owner of the huge bookselling operation that is set to wipe out her business. And yet these two polar opposites find they have something deeper and more essential in common. And, of course, that inexplicable ingredient: chemistry.

Your task today is twofold. Firstly, make a list of romcoms you've loved; then, for each, work out how the pairing works and why. What is it that means these two people are both the perfect rivals, opposites or enemies and what conversely makes them the perfect lovers? What are the magic ingredients?

Then write three 'book-jacket blurb' premises of your own, based on these principles. Give us your best romcom pitches. And then, if you're inspired, go and write one. It could be the next big-hitter.

# 20th May

"When you're writing a book, with people in it as opposed
to animals, it is no good having people who are ordinary,
because they are not going to interest your readers at all.
Every writer in the world has to use the characters that have
something interesting about them, and this is even more true
in children's books."

Roald Dahl

Today we're making up characters. Taking inspiration from Roald
Dahl's notion that characters ought to be extraordinary, here's your
task.

Make a list of five jobs. Pick jobs that give your characters some
interest; for example, a zookeeper has more potential than
a supermarket checkout operator, because they exist in a world that's
more exotic and unusual.

Next, give them a name and a backstory. Where are they from? Do
they have family? How did they end up here? Do they have any
secrets?

Now, give them some detail, some quirks and flaws. What motivates
them? What do they believe in? What do they want? And finally,
write a one-line premise for a story for each character, in which we
meet them and set off on a journey. What is the problem that they
are challenged by and how do they embark on their adventure? How
will they change?

# 21st May

*"The process is always the same. I get an inspiration for a new song, I put it down on paper immediately so I won't lose it. When I am ready to go to the studio with it, I play it a few times on the piano and edit, add, and type the lyrics and take it to the studio."*
Yoko Ono

It's **National Memo Day** – so here's your task. You will need a pile of Post-it notes. If you don't have any, cut up a piece of paper into the equivalent squares.

A memo is a reminder: a short note to prompt an action, to tell you to do something, or perhaps to instruct an annoying housemate in a passive-aggressive way ('Not your milk!').

Your task today is to imagine that a bin blows over in the street, and out of it falls a whole bunch of Post-its from a block of flats – all from different flats – each scribbled with a memo. Write the notes from a range of characters; maybe some by the granny on the seventeenth floor, others between teenaged lovers, one from a dad to his son, you get the picture…

Use this to build a sense of the community that lives in the building. Now, picking your favourite protagonists from these memos, write a scenario in which two of them have an altercation or a game-changing interaction in their building. Feel free to bring in other characters from the block if they want to get involved too. They often do, they're a nosy bunch.

# 22nd May

To mark the birthday of **Sir Arthur Conan Doyle,** Sherlock Holmes's creator, let's jump into his world of the investigative thriller and play the great 'consulting detective' for the day.

Your task is to write the opening scene of a new detective mystery. In your set-up, a body is discovered. Set your scene clearly – you can have fun with where and when this might take place. Detective stories are often set in glamorous eras, in castles or on international train journeys. It's often a glitzy and expensive world that would be fun to write, so go for gold!

Set up some morsels of delicious information – clues, which your detective will spot in order to send them off on their investigation. People your scene with potential suspects. If you can, read a couple of detective story opening scenes to give you ideas. Whilst you don't have to follow any particular rules, this could help you find the sort of language and means of capturing tension that will give your mystery the sense of a thriller. And then give it a title: *The Case of the…*

# 23rd May

"Sometimes words need music too. Sometimes the descriptions are not enough. Books should be written with soundtracks, like films."
Terry Pratchett

I want you to think about the musical world of your writing. There are two types of music in film: *diegetic* and *non-diegetic*, both derived from the literary term 'diegesis'.

Diegetic music is 'in scene', i.e. music within the story that the characters can hear. It's on the radio they are listening to; sung in a club where they are dancing. Non-diegetic music is music that the audience can hear but the characters cannot, used to enhance the emotional world of the story. It's the score, the soundtrack, the violins that swell when the lovers run into each other's arms.

Your task today is to take one of the following scenes as your source:

- A scene you've written recently, perhaps as a task from this book.

- A scene that you like from a film or play that exists.

- Or write a brand-new scene to play with for this exercise.

Now, choose some non-diegetic music to play over your scene. Consider what the emotional tone is and what sort of music could enhance that. Richard Curtis uses pop music in a lot of his work to reveal something about the characters, and to give his films and air of fun and nostalgia. Perhaps you want sweeping strings and classical romance; perhaps you'll use heavy metal to drive the action home. Try reading your scene out with a couple of options playing in the background – which works best? Is it what you expected? Sometimes a wild card can add something new and surprising to a scene you thought you knew really well.

Now put that music to the side. This time, I'd like you to write music into the scene as part of the story. This will help move your scene from being wholly dialogue-based to something more layered and sonorous. See how the action of engaging (or not) with the music develops the characters.

Next time you're writing, keep these tools in mind and perhaps try to write more music into your work. Or try playing music as you're writing and see what that does to the story.

MAY

# 24th May

*"It is only natural to pattern yourself after someone...*
*But you can't just copy someone. If you like someone's work,*
*the important thing is to be exposed to everything that*
*person has been exposed to."*
Bob Dylan

To celebrate **Bob Dylan's birthday**, we're going to take some inspiration from his tip and deep-dive into a favourite writer's work. Which writer do you admire? Now, give yourself half an hour (at least) to sit and read their work. Ideally read a variety. It's better to read the opening pages of four Jane Austen novels than an entire chapter of one. (Or the opening of all six. She only wrote six, it won't take you long.) Scribble down why this work makes your heart sing. What specifically do you find compelling about it?

Now try to write a couple of paragraphs in that writer's style. Just try. Attempt to be as accurate as you can in following their syntax, language choices, style and form. Drink in everything about how they write, and – just this once (don't make a habit of it) – copy them. It's one way to learn very directly how skilled they are... particularly as it will inevitably become obvious that they're not easy to copy. Such is genius. But by identifying the qualities in their work, you can keep these in mind when writing your own.

# 25th May

*"Imagination is more important than knowledge.
For knowledge is limited to all we know and understand, while
imagination embraces the entire world, and all there ever will
be to know and understand."*
Albert Einstein

Time for a game. Let's play word association. Set a timer for ten minutes. Now write down a word you love. Now write down a great word that relates to this word. And then a fabulous word that relates to this last word. Either by theme, sound, rhyme, notion, however you like. Then do it again. And again.

You're making a long list of interrelated excellent words – but remember your latest word *only* needs to relate to the word before, not the list as a whole, so it can twist and turn in any direction and should soon move far away from your original starting point. Here's an example:

*Perennial – Bloom – Wild – Rugged – Hunk – Cheese – Pop – Weasel – Squeasy – Bottle – Frobscottle…*

Keep writing for ten minutes. Then have a look at your fabulous list – and try to use more words like this in your writing.

# 26th May

*"The Beatles saved the world from boredom."*
George Harrison

The Beatles released *Sgt. Pepper's Lonely Hearts Club Band* on this day in 1967. What an album. And what an album cover. The image, created by Jann Haworth and Peter Blake, is now universally known and even won its own Grammy. A composite picture, featuring the four Beatles in brightly coloured suits, surrounded by a cast of vibrant characters from history and literature.

Your task is to have a good look at this cover picture, pick three of the characters, and stick them in a scene. There are plenty of lists online as to who's who in the picture. Here are a few to choose from: Carl Jung (psychiatrist), Fred Astaire (actor and dancer), Oscar Wilde (writer), Aleister Crowley (occultist), Mae West (actress), Bob Dylan (musician), Dylan Thomas (poet), Sri Mahavatar Babaji (Hindu guru), Lewis Carroll (writer), Shirley Temple (actress). It's rather a shame that there aren't a more diverse group of women represented but there you go, it was the sixties.

Put your chosen three characters into a scene that involves one of the props on the cover. These include a hookah (smoking pipe), a horn, a trophy, a nine-inch television set, a cloth doll, a garden gnome and an idol statue of the Hindu goddess Lakshmi. Those are your ingredients. Off you go.

# 27th May

*"It has become increasingly plain to me that the very excellent organisation of a long book or the finest perceptions and judgment in time of revision do not go well with liquor. A short story can be written on the bottle, but for a novel you need the mental speed that enables you to keep the whole pattern inside your head and ruthlessly sacrifice the sideshows... I would give anything if I hadn't written Part III of* Tender is the Night *entirely on stimulant."*
F. Scott Fitzgerald

On this day in 1922, 'The Curious Case of Benjamin Button' by F. Scott Fitzgerald was published. It's a story in which, as the protagonist's life progresses, he gets younger, as everyone else gets older. This, of course, means that even though he is 'born' as an old man, he has the mind and curiosity of a child. And then, as time passes, though he is getting physically younger, he gains life experience and knowledge, and will ultimately be at his most experienced when he is youngest. This deliciously inventive idea gives the author the opportunity to explore the themes of time, age, love and family in a unique and imaginative way.

Use that today as your inspiration for a piece of writing, in which your protagonist has to deal with living their life in reverse.

# 28th May

*"Never say 'no' to adventures. Always say 'yes',
otherwise you'll lead a very dull life."*
Ian Fleming

Today, you are going to write three lists, as follows: People, Places and Things. These are, by the by, the three triggers for addiction, as explored in Duncan Macmillan's brilliant play of that title (definitely worth reading – it is an astonishing piece of work). But today we're using these three words simply as a playful way into an imaginative exercise, which doesn't require being serious at all.

In each category, write twenty-five examples. For example:

- People: a surgeon, a tropical explorer, a corpse, a Michelin-starred chef.

- Places: an elevator, a wormhole in space, a worm hole in the garden, an underground bunker, inside a person's ear canal.

- Things: a cheese grater, a train ticket, a bottle of absinthe, an original Klimt painting.

When you're done, cut these lists up and make three piles. Pick one from each at random and give yourself ten minutes to write a creative response, using your three elements. Repeat this three times. See what bubbles up.

# 29th May

*"Creativity is a wild mind and a disciplined eye."*
Dorothy Parker

Speaking of discipline, let's talk about movies. Specifically, writer Joseph Campbell's definiteion of movie structure: 'The Hero's Journey'. He created a nine-step plan to summarise what the typical 'journey' involves. By creating a story that adheres to these guidelines, a writer should, in theory, be able to create a twisty-turny, high-stakes, emotionally engaging, dramatically satisfying story arc. Let's try it. Fill in his plan below, designing a classic, archetypal plot as you go.

1.  In an ordinary world... (i.e. the world of your hero 'before' an event changes everything)

2.  A flawed protagonist... (describe them and tell us what their flaw is – this will inevitably become the personal problem that your hero has to overcome, so make it an interesting one)

3.  A catalytic event happens...

4.  After taking stock... (what must the hero do to right this wrong, solve this problem)

5.  The hero commits to action... (the journey)

6.  The stakes get raised... (everything gets harder and more dramatic)

7.  The hero must learn a lesson... (see point 2... what is your hero's flaw? How are they going to rise up to overcome it?)

8.  To stop the antagonist... (ideally external *and* internal, i.e. the baddie/the force/the outside problem your hero has to wrestle with *and* the emotional hurdle they have to overcome)

9.  To achieve their goal... (and restore the world/win the girl/ become a better human)

# 30th May

It's **National Creativity Day**. So today we're going to do something a bit different. I want you to choose an alternative art form in which to tell a story. It could be drawing. Making a collage, a sculpture, a song, a composition, a piece of clothing, an artistic cake. Your task is to tell a story or create a character in this alternative form…

So, for example, if you want to make a cake, do it from a character's point of view, so it might be in the mode of a posh French Queen of Patisseries, a Parisian madame whose first love is sugar and the wickedly creative things you can do with it. Or you might make a character sculpture out of found objects in the garden. Or write a song in the voice of an Arctic explorer. Just keep the idea of story in mind as you're working. What does your artwork tell us? What story are you telling?

# 31st May

*"I did the traditional thing with falling in love with words, reading books and underlining lines I liked and words I didn't know. It was something I always did."*
Carrie Fisher

For today's task I want you to find a thesaurus and pick twenty words that you don't know. Choose meaty, delicious words, full-fat and flavourful.

For each one, write down its definition in your own words, and find four synonyms for it, to help embed its meaning in your brain. This way you'll start thinking *around* these words and will be more likely to use them in the future.

Maybe write them in colourful pen and stick them near your desk. You might even want to add a new word each day, to expand your writer's arsenal of fabulous words.

# June

# 1st June

Time for more writer training.

We're going to do another HIIT class to get your writing muscles souped up like Schwarzenegger.

Set a timer and do each of the following for *two minutes*, as many as you can in the time:

1. Write a list of adjectives beginning with 'S' (slippery, soulful, surreptitious, sombre…).

2. Write a list of girls' names beginning with 'K'.

3. Write a list of verbs (doing words) beginning with 'B' (burrow, bounce, beautify…).

4. Write a list of words associated with the summer.

5. Write a list of stinky words.

6. Write a list of all the words you can think of that end in '-ful'.

7. Write a list of fictional sports – the more ludicrous they sound, the better.

JUNE

# 2nd June

Today it's **Thomas Hardy's birthday.** One of his daily practices was to write in tremendous depth about everyday things… items or activities we'd often consider boring, but in great detail. It increased his observation skills, he said, and helped him see elements of life in a new light.

So today I'd like you to pick something very mundane – part of an everyday routine. It could be brushing your teeth, tying your shoes, making a cup of tea. But write *every detail*. Think sensorially – all the sights, sounds, smells, sensations. Try to observe the specifics in a way you don't usually notice.

Your challenge is to make a boring activity utterly captivating.

JUNE

# 3rd June

*"The only thing that can save the world is the reclaiming of the awareness of the world. That's what poetry does."*
Allen Ginsberg

In celebration of **Allen Ginsberg's birthday** we're going to write a Beat poem. The Beat generation were a group of artists writing in America in the 1940s and '50s – Ginsberg and his pals Jack Kerouac, Diane di Prima and Michael McClure. Their work was a rebellion against formulaic 'conventional' writing forms, in which writers worked to draft and redraft their poetry to fit specific forms. Instead, they lived by the mantra 'First idea, best idea', and tended to write freestyle, without editing themselves. Their poems often explored themes of freedom, disenfranchisement in the post-World War II period, the American experience, and the nature of love and meaning. Allan Ginsberg's 'Howl' is one of the most famous Beat poems.

So today, you're going to write a poem in their style. It should be written spontaneously, without self-censorship or editing – it is not meant to be perfect, it's meant to be *authentic*. Your poem should be an instant reaction to whatever you are observing. Punctuation can go out the window, it's a free-written, long-sentenced stream-of-consciousness poem, so don't limit yourself.

Your subject is 'Awareness'. That's your only instruction. That's it! Go!

JUNE

# 4th June

Today's simple writing prompt is to write about someone embarking on a life-changing journey. It could be you, from lived experience. Or you in a fantasy. Or a fictional character, set at any time, going to any place.

Your task is to capture the thrill of setting off, the embarkation, the beginnings of a new adventure. The trepidation about heading into the unknown, and the excitement about what might come…

Then, if you're inspired, book a ticket to somewhere *fabulous* and do the journey for real. I dare you.

# 5th June

*"I always do my draft in long hand
because even the ink is part of the flow."*
Martin Amis

Today, open a recipe book. Find a recipe that you find interesting. It could be the ingredients. It could be the style of writing or the origin of the meal.

Now that meal is going to become the focus of your scene. Choose who is making it, who is eating it, in what context, and what plays out over the course of the meal. Who might find themselves eating this and why? Try and include the sensuous details of the food in your tale.

JUNE

# 6th June

*"Memory is the diary that we all carry about with us."*
Oscar Wilde

In early June 2017 Inua Ellams' brilliant play **Barber Shop Chronicles** was published in a revised version. If you were lucky enough to see it, it was a real treat. Written in verse, Inua's play is set across five African cities and London, chartering the encounters, routines and rituals of life in the barbershops that were a feature of Inua's upbringing. Places of chat and banter, wise counsel and life advice, a visit to the barbershop was much more than just a haircut.

Think about the places that were important to you – and part of your culture – growing up. Perhaps it was a local library, a drama group, the laundrette, a corner café, the local swimming pool. Where could you see – and learn about – life within a community?

Choose a place from your own past and write a scene set there – in verse, if you like. Use the juxtaposition of a practical routine (choosing a haircut, ordering tea, reserving a library book) with observations of life and a greater sense of what this place means within the community. See if you can capture the specific way the people talk to each other within the poetry. If you want inspiration, do get hold of a copy of Inua's play; it is a brilliant read.

# 7th June

*"Attention to detail – like the right words and notes in the right places – that makes the difference between a good song and a great song."*
Prince

Today, to celebrate **Prince's birthday,** write a passage that features as many as possible of the following items/ideas, each the title of a Prince song. You must include at least three, and you get extra points if you manage all of them:

- A raspberry beret
- A kiss
- A little red Corvette
- Purple rain
- Cream
- Starfish and coffee
- Pink cashmere
- Alphabet Street

# 8th June

*"Man cannot discover new oceans*
*unless he has the courage to lose sight of the shore."*
André Gide

'Show, don't tell.' It's an excellent mantra to live by as a dramatist. It's often best for a character to communicate how they're feeling through action rather than words. To take someone's hand as a quiet symbol of forgiveness is a more powerful image on stage than the character simply saying, 'I forgive you.'

So, for today's task, write a scene for two characters with a strong emotion at the heart of it, but where the characters don't articulate their feelings at any point. Instead, choose an activity for them to do, revealing their feelings through the way they do it. Maybe they're trying to cook a meal together, or do the washing, or navigate a route. Choose a palpable emotional subtext (i.e. they are breaking up, they are getting together, there's an unspoken secret) and have a go. Really enjoy letting the specific ways they behave *physically* tell us everything about what's going on in their relationship.

# 9th June

Here's an exercise after Pinter's own heart. Write a scene for three characters, named A, B and C. A is trapped in a room by B and C and needs to work out why and how to get out. In the room there's a window, two doors and a trapdoor.

Try to capitalise on the non-specific nature of the set-up (i.e. the characters don't even have names) in the way you write the scene. Specifically, avoid overexplaining – we don't need to know *who* these characters are, or even why they are there… the aim is to create a tension-filled, atmospheric scene where we can enjoy squirming as B and C put A in a compromising scenario.

Harold Pinter was a master of building suspense, often by keeping his dialogue as sparse and elusive as possible. It's much more captivating not to know too much, to keep the mystery alive.

JUNE

# 10th June

*"A playwright must be his own audience.*
*A novelist may lose his readers for a few pages;*
*a playwright never dares lose his audience for a minute."*
Terence Rattigan

Happy birthday, **Terence Rattigan**. The great playwright primarily wrote populist comedies, written very much for the 'everyman', to be accessible to everyone... plays that his proverbial 'Aunt Edna' would like (his way of describing the idea of a general middle-class, 'regular' audience).

Yet he also wrote deeply serious plays, several of which were perhaps autobiographical. Those plays focused on a character's interior world: understated emotions set against the backdrop of a wider political landscape. He achieved this on the stage through carefully crafted, restrained dialogue, which allowed an audience to understand a character's truth by observing what's *not* said. He believed drama was the best form for such stories as they allowed the unspoken to play out live, between actors, in front of an audience. That's the magic of theatre as a form.

Today, let's look at the difference between plays and novels, and consider why certain stories work best in one than the other. Write a list of your favourite plays and novels, then consider why each works in that specific form.

What is it, do you think, that defines a story appropriate for a novel as opposed to a play? Is it to do with the shape of the story? The scale of it? The timeline? The nature of the narrative (so an internal story in which we spend a great deal of time with a quiet characters' thoughts might be harder to play out in the dialogue-based medium of a play)? The tone? The setting?

Now write a list of five ideas for plays and five ideas for novels, stick it on your wall, and, one day, write one.

# 11th June

Write a list of the thirty most beautiful words you can think of. What makes them so exquisite? Is it the meaning of the words? Or their sound? The way they feel when you say them? Long, warm, delicious vowel sounds, or bright, sparkly, poppy plosives? Spend time putting your list together, there are some wonderfully mellifluous, sonorous words to choose from.

Then, inspired by your list, make up ten new beautiful words and their meanings, using the characteristics you found in your first choices to inspire your own creations.

JUNE

# 12th June

*"I can shake off everything as I write;
my sorrows disappear, my courage is reborn."*
Anne Frank

On this day in 1942, **Anne Frank** was given a diary for her birthday.

Your task today is to write a diary entry for a character of your choosing. Pick someone (or invent someone) whose life is wildly different from your own and think about what they might want to write.

A diary is a wonderful way into a character because it contains a meeting of both the action of their lives – what they are doing, day by day – and their secret thoughts. Consider this when deciding whose diary you'd like to write. To give you a clue, think about whose diary you might like to read – and dive in!

# 13th June

Today, pick the title of one of the following Alanis Morrisette songs as a title for a passage of prose. Write in the first person as a woman who has something to say and is pretty opinionated (and kick-ass) about it. She might also be a little bit angry, which is no bad thing.

- 'Head Over Feet'

- 'Reasons I Drink'

- 'Hand in My Pocket'

- 'Not the Doctor'

- '21 Things I Want in a Lover'

# 14th June

*"At the end, we're kind of observers – creative people,
I mean. I feel like an observer, and I'm pretty much able to
step out of things and see how things are playing out."*
Nick Cave

Nick Cave is a pretty inspirational guy. He describes the way he comes up with songs as almost subconscious – waiting for the song to come from the outside so he can catch it, rather than brewing from inside him. He says:

> *'My advice to you is to change your basic relationship to song-writing… You are not the "Great Creator" of your songs, you are simply their servant, and the songs will come to you when you have adequately prepared yourself to receive them. They are not inside you, unable to get out; rather, they are outside of you, unable to get in. Songs, in my experience, are attracted to an open, playful and motivated mind.'*

So, in an attempt to have some Cave-like inspiration, I want you to find a comfortable place to lie on the floor (or on a couch if you'd rather). You are going to close your eyes and wait for a story idea to come to you. Try to empty your head and be open to random thoughts arriving. If you start thinking about practical stuff like what to eat for dinner, politely move that thought on and go back to your relaxed state of openness. Stay there until an interesting thought arrives – an idea that can, and will, become a story. Then write it down. Voilà – thanks, Nick!

# 15th June

*"Make your own dream."*
John Lennon

Today let's take some inspiration from The Beatles as a writing prompt, using ideas from their songs as our toolkit.

- Pick two characters from the following list: Bungalow Bill, Eleanor Rigby, Dizzy Miss Lizzy, The Fool on the Hill, Her Majesty, Lady Madonna.

- Now pick a place: Abbey Road, Helter Skelter, Blue Jay Way, Strawberry Fields, Kansas City.

- Now pick an object: Yellow Submarine, Maxwell's Silver Hammer, Rubber Soul, Glass Onion, Matchbox.

- Now pick a title: 'Help!', 'The Night Before', 'She Came In Through the Bathroom Window', 'A Taste of Honey', 'Yesterday'.

There are your ingredients, now time to fry them up together. Write either a poem, a scene or a prose passage using the elements you chose above, each of which comes from the inventive, lyrical work of The Beatles.

# 16th June

Today, you're going to write a recipe in character. Pick your dish and write the recipe in a way that tells us more about the chef's personality than it does about how to cook the dish. Who is cooking here? A professional chef, a bon vivant? A grandma doling out a family recipe? An impatient matron at a boarding school? What's their attitude to the food? To their audience? To the act of eating? Is it seductive? Romantic? Glutinous? Rigid?

For extra deliciousness, pick a recipe that highlights the character's nature... someone trying to seduce us with a tantalising recipe is far more likely to be cooking something indulgent and moist than hot dogs.

# 17th June

Today we're going to do short, sharp writing shocks. Give yourself forty-five seconds on the timer to do each of the following.

Forty-five seconds doesn't give you enough time to plan; it hardly gives you time to think at all (and not much time to write). Good luck!

1. Write an argument between a zookeeper and a monkey.

2. Write a statement protesting your innocence for a dastardly crime.

3. Write a love poem to your childhood sweetheart.

4. Write a maths equation for how to square the circle of an isosceles triangle.

5. Write a recipe for Vietnamese Bo La Lot noodles (without googling it).

6. Write a complaint letter.

7. Write a hymn to a god of your choice.

8. Write a romcom set in Paris.

# 18th June

Let's design a character by playing *'Why?'* You need to begin with a character name and one character trait. For example, my character is called Mabel Fritz, and she is cripplingly agoraphobic (scared of leaving the house).

Now set your timer for ten minutes and begin asking 'Why?' as follows:

*Why is Mabel Fritz cripplingly shy?*

Now answer the question in a single line:

*Because she was traumatised by a cow when she was a kid.*

Now ask 'Why?' again:

*Why was she traumatised by a cow when she was a kid?*

*Because she tried to make friends with it and got bitten.*

*Why did she try to make friends with the cow?*

*Because she didn't have any human friends.*

*Why didn't she have any human friends?*

*Because they all died.*

*Why did they all die?*

*Because they all got a plague.*

*Why did they all get a plague?*

*Because they all drank the water, except for Mabel.*

*Why didn't Mabel drink the water?*

*Because...* etc.

Without having to think too much, suddenly we have a character with a pretty rapidly forming, fully fledged backstory. See how far you can get with yours in ten minutes, and if you feel inspired, carry on!

JUNE

# 19th June

*"Being in the same room with people
and creating something together is a good thing."*
Robin Williams

Robin Williams was right, it is a *wonderful* experience bouncing ideas off other people, rather than always embarking on the creative process solo. So today, you're going to get some contributions from the world outside you and me and this book.

Your task is to collect the following from other people:

- A character name.

- A characteristic for your character.

- A problem or question.

- A setting.

- A first line.

- An unexpected wild card – this can be an object, a second character, an extra dilemma, an abstract idea, a colour, a song… anything to add into the mix.

I want you to find these ideas from other people. If you have housemates/ a partner/friends/work colleagues, ask them. Ideally get different items from different people to make it as much of a mix as possible.

If you're really stuck and for some reason you have no friends, no colleagues and you shun human company in all its forms, then google each of the above categories and pull them off the internet. But the key factor is *you* are not choosing – the variables are given to you by the gods of creativity (or your housemates).

Now your task is to write a story that's no longer than a single page using all the elements you've been given. There you go. Teamwork makes the dream work.

# 20th June

*"Beware the lollipop of mediocrity;*
*lick it once and you'll suck forever."*
Brian Wilson

Brian Wilson may have won at weird life lessons with the quote above. We're going to try to give him a run for his money. Today your task is to write ten 'fridge magnet' slogans, but each using something unexpected.

For each to work, you need a life lesson to impart… some trite pop-psychology statement about how to live your life freely, or love your friends, or reach for the stars, or open your heart or whatever naff-orism you fancy.

But rather than going for full-on cheese, choose a random object like Wilson's lollipop. Maybe a cheese grater? An ironing board? A wooden spoon? And write your slogan using this as the active object. I can guarantee that whatever you write is already going to be more creative and meaningful than anything you can buy in a high-street greetings-card emporium.

# 21st June

*"Personally, I don't take holidays; I go on trips.*
*My idea of relaxing is taking a trip that isn't commissioned.*
*I'll work just as hard, but without that nagging pressure of*
*fulfilling a commission. Now that's what I call a holiday."*
Martin Parr

Today is the **Summer Solstice**: the longest day of the year and the official start of summer. Hoorah!

So it's time to go on a trip to celebrate! Let's go and get some inspiration from elsewhere – and make the most of this lovely time. Get out of the house and take yourself somewhere you weren't planning to go today. Even if it's just for fifteen minutes. When you get there, write a short piece inspired by what you observe around you. I hope, by chance, you have the whole day off and can get some distance from home, to escape into a surprising new setting.

In its simplest form, this can be observing a person in the café/park/subway/post office and writing a short monologue for them. Or, if you've got more time, go and hang out in a museum, or take a train to the seaside. Get to know one of the objects or paintings – or observe a fisherman, or what you will – and write something inspired by what you see.

# 22nd June

*"You don't start out writing good stuff.*
*You start out writing crap and thinking it's good stuff,*
*and then gradually you get better at it.*
*That's why I say one of the most valuable traits is persistence."*
Octavia E. Butler

The more we can get out of our own perspectives and comfort zones as writers, the better. We have to discard our own point of view and try to jump feet first into someone else's. Imagine everything we know and feel about the world is replaced with a wholly different point of view. That is the goal of creative character writing.

Have a look at the room you are in. Now think of a character who would be entirely out of place in this room. Someone who wouldn't know what to do with themselves here; who would find themselves completely out of their comfort zone.

Now write the scene in which they find themselves in this room with you, encountering it for the first time. What happens? Do they stay? How do you feel? What happens next?

# 23rd June

*"Every time you type something on a typewriter,
it is a one-of-a-kind work of art."*
Tom Hanks

Have you ever written on a typewriter? It's a *wholly* different writing experience to writing on a computer. Not only because it's slower, but it's really *really* difficult to delete anything. That means you have to write better the first time and think before you type – otherwise you have to type the whole damn thing again.

Bearing that in mind, today you're going to type a piece without going back to revise it. Choose from one of the following three first lines:

*'May I have a glass of Sancerre, and a Pouilly-Fumé for my daughter?'*

or

*'The last thing they expected was he turn up in a luminous hat.'*

or

*'"Frippletryrubourgafiy," the alien said, when I asked him.'*

Now continue the story, write for ten minutes, but think carefully about each line before you write it down. And work towards completing your story in a satisfying way before the time's up.

# 24th June

*"Every child is an artist,*
*the problem is staying an artist when you grow up."*
Pablo Picasso

Today we're going to start with a drawing. First, pick a country. Then pick a profession. Then pick an age (eighteen upwards). Then pick a gender... whatever that might mean to you – we're not attached to binary divisions here.

Now draw your Brazilian, eighty-year-old, non-binary acrobat, or whoever your character is. Fill the picture with as much detail as you can to get to know them as well as possible, through the task of drawing them: their expression, their physicality, their mood, their perspective.

Take a look at them. How's their day looking? What is the huge dilemma they are facing right now? (NB. There *is* a huge dilemma – this is going to be a dramatic story.)

Give yourself twenty minutes to write their story. Be clear about what their drama is and why they are in this position. Decide the tone you want to write in (is it comic, is it a mystery, a tragedy, a pastiche?) and set off on your mission.

# 25th June

*"Never use a long word where a short one will do."*
George Orwell

It's **George Orwell's birthday** today, so let's do an exercise as a nod to the great man, based on his 'Six Questions for Writing'. He was a passionately political guy who often wrote about issues he cared about, either in essays or fiction. So today, pick a topic that you feel passionately about. It could be a political issue, a local one, a family question, a social idea, an environmental topic. And write a page about it, spontaneously. Do this now before you read on.

Hello again. Now you've done that, take a look at Orwell's questions, as follows. He said:

*A scrupulous writer, in every sentence that he writes, will ask himself at least four questions, thus:*

1. *What am I trying to say?*

2. *What words will express it?*

3. *What image or idiom will make it clearer?*

4. *Is this image fresh enough to have an effect?*

*And he will probably ask himself two more:*

5. *Could I put it more shortly?*

6. *Have I said anything that is avoidably ugly?'*

Now return to your page of writing and go through these questions. Ask yourself each in turn for every sentence on your page, and edit your writing accordingly. See how much it's improved by giving it the Orwell treatment. It's a pretty good editing technique – though beware, don't be too hard on yourself: you may end up with nothing left!

JUNE

# 26th June

Write a list of all the characteristics that make you *you*. What defines you? What are your politics? What are your beliefs? What are your passions? What qualities do you have? What traits would you rather not admit to?

Now, look at this list and pick a *different* name, gender, profession and age from your own. This is a new character... with your characteristics. But they're not you. Write about a day in the life of this person, from their perspective, but trying to separate yourself from them.

By doing this, try to start using elements of who *you* are to inform the truth and detail of your writing, and yet simultaneously enjoy jumping into a different body and life to find an imaginative way into a new character. Combining these two skills is a great way to ensure deep yet creative writing.

# 27th June

*"My favourite thing is to go where I've never been."*
Diane Arbus

Writing location is a key part of creating a detailed creative landscape. So today, pick a place you've never been to. Somewhere you think sounds intriguing, that you'd love to visit. And google the bejeesus out of it. Find out everything you can about this place in as much detail as possible. Read articles, watch YouTube videos, search for photos. You are trying to get a sense of everything, from the temperature and the scents in the air to the sounds, the ambience, the music, the business, the people, the traffic, the history, the cultural landscape.

Now write a scene set in this location, using all this delicious detail to inform your writing. Within your scene, write one person who is new to the place, who is seeing it for the first time, and a second character who is a local. How does this interaction work? How much can you enjoy visiting this place through the fiction you're writing?

Remember going forward that research is an incredible tool as a writer. Often we can't visit the scenarios we write about – I'm currently writing an adaptation of a nineteenth-century novel and a film with a character from the moon in it. I haven't been to either – but through research I can have a good go at imagining.

# 28th June

*"Reading one book is like eating one potato chip."*
Diane Duane

Diane is right – a dearth of books is a great tragedy for any aspiring writer. We learn about writing from reading.

So today's task is to go to your local library – or bookshop if you're flash with the cash – and return with a selection of new reading material. Ideally some fiction, some autobiography (real lives teach us a lot about voice and story)… and maybe even a wildcard from a genre you'd never usually read. Try to read every day for the next month – even if it's just a page or so – and refill your literary well.

JUNE

# 29th June

*"The books I would like to print
are the books I love to read and keep."*
William Morris

Today pick a weather condition. Extremes are good. Write a description of a landscape being affected by this weather. For inspiration, take a look at the freezing conditions in Gogol's *The Overcoat*, the dry heat of *The Grapes of Wrath*, the effect of the summer in *The Go-Between*, or the mud in Dickens' *Bleak House*.

Through your description, discover a person in that landscape, and see what happens. Are they battling against it? Are they possessed by it? Does their life depend on it? Weather is so often imaginatively exercising and emotionally affecting. Drama can be ramped up if the characters are made uncomfortable, tense, irritated or vulnerable by extreme temperatures. So pick your climate condition accordingly and then turn up (or down) the heat for added drama.

# 30th June

*"I started writing these love songs to myself.
Dudes come and go, they'll break your heart –
I could never break my own heart."*
Lizzo

Time for more writer brain training. Do these to get your writing muscles activated.

Set a timer and do each of the following for *two minutes*, as many as you can in the time:

1. Write a list of adjectives beginning with 'B' (buoyant, benevolent…).

2. Write a list of character names beginning with 'S' (famous ones or make them up).

3. Write a list of verbs beginning with 'T' (trick, tackle…).

4. Write a list of words you associate with childhood.

5. Write a list of sensual words.

6. Write a list of all the words you can think of that include 'tion'.

# July

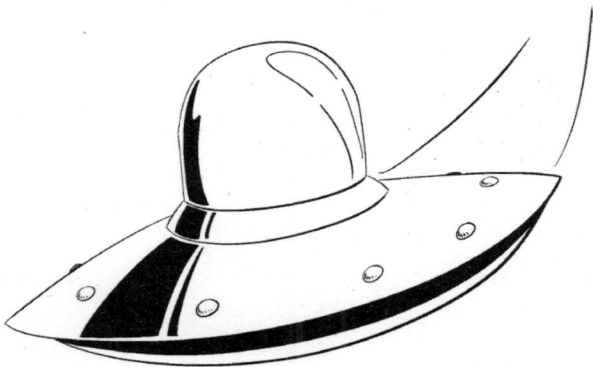

# 1st July

*"Always laugh when you can, it is cheap medicine."*
Lord Byron

As it's **International Joke Day**, you're going to write some funny stuff. No pressure. The good thing is you don't have to share it with anyone (unless you want to) – so you can just have fun. And that's the best way to find your funny.

There are lots of tropes in comic writing: use of wit, irony, anecdote, one-liners, punchlines, reversals at the end of a line, contradictory afterthoughts, puns, unspoken truths. Some of these we assume are innate: the ability to be witty, for example. But don't panic – there are lot of tricks to 'up the funny' in your writing.

Let's cut ourselves a bit of slack and begin with something easy-ish. A good deal of comedy comes from incongruence, i.e. juxtaposing two things that crash against each other. Two contrasting views can lead to a misunderstanding (google the 'four candles/fork handles' sketch by the Two Ronnies – genius). Or you can subvert an expectation, by taking a well-known phrase or cliché and flipping it.

For example: *'The first time I met my wife, I knew she was a keeper. She was wearing massive gloves.'* Alun Cochrane's joke makes us think we're heading for romance – but nope – it's about football.

Or *'She got her looks from her father. He was a plastic surgeon.'* The ever-brilliant Groucho Marx.

Or this cliché, rewritten in a flip-reverse, by Roseanne Barr: *'My mother says the best way to a man's heart is through his stomach. I'd say it's straight through his chest.'* Deliciously bloodthirsty when we think it's going to be sentimental.

The more that the flipped statement stands in opposition to the first, the better, i.e. love versus murder here. Back to Marx again: *'I've had a wonderful evening. But this wasn't it.'*

So your task is this: Write a list of ten clichés. Romantic ones are a good place to begin. Then find a way to change the end of the line, or add an addendum that contradicts the tone. Have a go, then have a second look and see if you can be funnier. Short and pithy is the best; long-winded is never funny. And the more contrast – i.e. the less romantic – the better.

Here are some phrases you could use to get you started:

- They say absence makes the heart grow fonder...

- My mum always said I'd know when I met 'the one'...

- I love her to the moon and back...

- He was my knight in shining armour...

- You are the apple of my eye...

- I always dreamed that one day I'd meet the perfect man...

- You have the key to my heart...

- It was love at first sight...

- They say love comes when you least expect it...

- I always thought that love made the world go round...

# 2nd July

*"I believe alien life is quite common in the universe, although intelligent life is less so. Some say it has yet to appear on planet Earth."*
Stephen Hawking

When I was little I was *obsessed* with UFOs. I mean, I grew up in the eighties and nineties with *The X-Files* and *E.T.* in my orbit, so it's hardly surprising. The tantalising idea that there might be someone, or something, out there was too deliciously compelling to resist for an overimaginative kid.

Today – **World UFO Day** – your task is to write a scene in which someone encounters an alien. But *avoiding all clichés*. Choose an unlikely character or personality for your alien. Avoid the large-black-eyed, oval-faced 'bad' aliens from sci-fi tropes... go for something you've never seen in the movies.

For inspiration, there's a truly original version of an alien encounter in Ted Chiang's short story 'Story of Your Life', which was adapted into the beautiful film *Arrival* by Denis Villeneuve. Worth both a watch and a read.

If you fancy it, you might begin by sketching your alien. Are they strange looking, and if so, how? Do they look like us? Do they have a body at all?

# 3rd July

Today, write a list of words. Words that make you spark, that have an intense effect on you, that epitomise your 'most intense obsessions'. Words that make you feel good feelings, bad feelings, that provoke a reaction, that stir a memory.

Set a timer for five minutes and write as many as you can. Then pin the list somewhere you can see it – and perhaps something in your compelling, provocative collection of words will be inspiration for a new story.

# 4th July

*"I like flawed characters, and I like seeing people who are supposed to be not villains but antagonists. There are elements to them, which are really annoying, but you kind of see where they came from. You see the things that caused those inadequacies."*
Taika Waititi

Today you're going to create a compelling antagonist. To do so, you have to avoid the trap of making them a two-dimensional 'baddie'. It's essential to find their humanity. You need to work out why they react the way they do, what in their past set them off on this path, and why they have what others might see as destructive traits. It's great territory for invention – look at the wealth of movies recently (*Cruella, Joker, Maleficent*) that have taken a classic 'baddie' and told the story from their perspective.

A good antagonist has hidden depths. They need a *reason* for being antagonistic: a strong motivation based on genuine feelings, e.g. something traumatic happened to them to make them act as they do. What run-in did young Cruella have with a Dalmatian to make her want to turn them into fur coats? What happened to the wolf that made him so determined to eat small girls in red coats? Fear, revenge or ambition are excellent qualities in the construction of an anti-hero's personality.

Your task today is to choose an infamous 'baddie' from a classic book or film, and to imagine what made them bad. Write a passage or scene that captures the incident that turned them into their current antagonistic persona. Take them on a journey from the 'before' to 'after', showing the catalyst to their transformation. And take this lesson with you: that any character in any story ought to be three-dimensional – and if they're not, give them a backstory.

# 5th July

*"All fiction is about people, unless it's about rabbits pretending to be people. It's all essentially characters in action, which means characters moving through time and changes taking place, and that's what we call 'the plot'."*
Margaret Atwood

Margaret Atwood's right (surprise, surprise… she *certainly* knows what she's doing in story terms). Characters need clear motivation in order to create action that propels the plot. So today we're going to build on yesterday's 'antagonist' exercise, in which you wrote an active backstory for a famous villain. Today we are going one better: you're going to come up with your own villain.

Think of a scenario where there's a conventional 'goodie' and 'baddie'. The baddie needs to possess characteristics that make them unappealing to a reader: a miserly sourpuss, the traffic warden who insists on clamping the car of the woman in labour, the pickpocket stealing from a child, the hostage-taker, the vindictive teacher. Write the outline of the scene. Now consider how you can flip it and write the scene fully (either as prose or as drama) but from the baddie's perspective, revealing why they behave in such a dastardly way. This is their backstory in action. Through your scene, we should come to understand the baddie, and if not like, at least empathise with them, forcing the reader to question their assumptions and understand our baddie's humanity.

# 6th July

*"If you have a good story idea, don't assume it must form a prose narrative. It may work better as a play, a screenplay or a poem. Be flexible."*
Hilary Mantel

**Hilary Mantel**, born on this day, was a writer extraordinaire. She wrote vivid, often historical, fiction, but despite her deep knowledge of the complicated political worlds she wrote about, she never overburdened her work with weighty information *just to show her research*. It's why so much historical fiction is so achingly dull, because its writers become obsessed with a subject, learn loads of facts about it, and shove it all into their prose at the expense of momentum and plot.

Not so Hilary. Her books are driven by plot. And she knew how to edit. One of her best tips to other writers was: '*First paragraphs can often be struck out. Are you performing a haka, or just shuffling your feet?*' It's a great reminder to jump into a scene as late as you can. We don't need the preamble.

Start with a family dinner at which there's going to be an explosive conversation. An admission of something. A revelation. The exposé of a secret. Begin by writing the long version of your scene, from the arrival of the family members, perhaps the preparation of food, the build-up, the seating, the serving, the explosion, the aftermath.

Now look at it again and try getting rid of paragraph one. Do you need it? Pull out any detail that you can't live without, then get rid of the rest of the paragraph. Now have a look at the new paragraph. Do you *really* need it? Try reading your piece without it. How late into the drama might this story start? Less isn't always more, but experiment to see where the happy medium is. Then do the same to the end of the scene, working backwards. Try leaving at the climactic point, no later. Is it more satisfying as a result?

# 7th July

*"Characters are the key to a good book.
It took me several novels to comprehend that."*
Michael Morpurgo

Choose one of your favourite characters from a book or film. Now write down all the reasons why you chose them.

For example, I enjoy the eponymous heroine of *Elinor Oliphant is Completely Fine* by Gail Honeyman. I love that she's an awkward misfit, an underdog, friendless, socially rude; that she wears the same clothes and eats the same meals every day because she finds it challenging to disrupt her routine. But she has a big heart. And she wants a friend.

Now take your list of characteristics and apply them to a new character. Elinor is a Scottish woman, twenty-nine years old, who works as a finance clerk for a graphic design company. So my new character might be a teenage boy, or a very old man, for example, from Hawaii, who makes sun hats for a living. What's important is that these characteristics (in my example, to be antisocial but desperate for a friend) are what make the character attractive.

Give your new character some background information, being sure to avoid anything that makes them anything like your starter character. Create their name, age, location, the time period when they're living, where they live and with whom, what's going on in their lives, why they are the way they are, and so on. Then write the first page of a novel about them. Go!

# 8th July

*"Analysis kills spontaneity. The grain once ground into flour springs and germinates no more."*
Henri-Frédéric Amiel

Here's a basic plot starter. Your task today is to write spontaneously, without overthinking or editing, enjoying the challenge of making it up as you go.

*A kid comes home from school to find a hole where his house was.*

# 9th July

*"Books are a form of political action. Books are knowledge. Books are reflection. Books change your mind."*
Toni Morrison

Sometimes the most everyday situations, when written about with wit, in detail, with thought and honesty, can be as touching as the greatest dramas.

Deborah Levy, for example, often reports relatively everyday activities in her series of life-writing novellas (*The Cost of Living*, *Things I Don't Want to Know* and *Real Estate*). Yet she does it with such a deft and personal tone – noticing detail in the familiar – that they read like beautiful invention.

Write about your morning this morning. Not all of it necessarily, that's up to you. Perhaps pick a moment, an encounter, or a task you did. Write with attention to detail, to fully engage the reader, drawing them in, allowing them to experience it as you did. The drama is in the detail. Throw the self-doubt to the side and trust that whatever happened is enough. And if nothing has happened, write about that.

# 10th July

*"I can't play bridge. I don't play tennis. All those things that people learn, and I admire, there hasn't seemed time for. But what there is time for is looking out the window."*
Alice Munro

On her birthday, follow the lead of **Alice Munro**: take ten minutes to stare out of the window. Set a timer. You can jot things down if you want, but I would recommend just letting yourself daydream.

Then whatever was in your head, write it down. Time and space to dream, to allow your mind to wander, are essential if you're going to live a creative life.

# 11th July

*"You never really understand a person until you consider things from his point of view. Until you climb inside of his skin and walk around in it."*

Harper Lee, *To Kill a Mockingbird*

Today is the anniversary of the publication of Harper Lee's mesmerising novel, ***To Kill a Mockingbird***. Your task today... go and buy a newspaper. Open it. On that page, select a person in it who you'd usually find frustrating, who you'd never choose to be friends with. Now try walking around in their shoes, as Lee wisely says.

What is it that annoys you about them and why might they be like that? What is tough for them? What might make them sad? Write a scene in which they're challenged by something that draws us in – and allows us to empathise with them. If you can do this about someone you really don't like, pretty soon you'll be able to write about anyone.

# 12th July

*"Let us pick up our books and our pens,
they are the most powerful weapons."*
Malala Yousafzai

Malala Yousafzai became famous for standing up for something she believed in passionately: the right to an education. Today is **Malala Day,** shining a light on the fact that many young women around the world are not able – or permitted – to go to school.

Today's task is to choose someone you find heroic (or make someone up, to represent an issue you care deeply about). Now, write a scene in which they make a speech, articulating their position, and showing their courageous side. Not a formal speech to a crowd, but a speech that comes spontaneously from an event that compels them to speak.

Perhaps it's a kid in the playground witnessing bullying, or someone protesting on a bus, or a spontaneous intervention in a station or on a street. Speeches that happen spontaneously are often much more dramatically engaging than a formal speech, because they come from a need to speak *in that moment.*

Try to balance the personal with the bigger picture: the situation between these specific people and the context of the global problem that their speech wrestles with. Micro and macro – often the jewels of a good speech.

# 13th July

*"Everybody walks past a thousand story ideas every day.
The good writers are the ones who see five or six of them.
Most people don't see any."*
Orson Scott Card

There are an endless number of potential stories. And you are full of them – I guarantee it! When asked to describe his songwriting process, Liam Gallagher explained that he imagined songs as buzzing around in the air, waiting to be plucked down and captured – you simply have to be ready and waiting to catch them. As Card suggests above, sometimes it's just about taking the time to look and think.

So here we go – let's come up with a list of creative ideas. Set a timer and write down as many ideas for stories as you possibly can in ten minutes. If you get stuck, think of a character and then stick them in a challenging situation. Remember that stories can take place in any time or universe; they can be major dramas or personal dilemmas. Write no more than one sentence for each idea. See how many you can come up with. Then, when you're done, underline your three favourites and let them jiggle around in your brain for the rest of the day.

# 14th July

*"Your intuition knows what to write, so get out of the way."*
Ray Bradbury

Whichever was your favourite idea from yesterday, write it. That's it!
Get out of your own way, don't overthink it, and maybe – hopefully –
it will write itself. You can choose whether to draw the idea as a
comic strip or write in prose. Or both!

JULY

# 15th July

*"One of the secrets of a happy life
is continuous small treats."*
Iris Murdoch

Today, it's **National Give Something Away Day** – so you're going to write something and send it to somebody. Perhaps a poem for your grandma. Perhaps a letter to a friend. Perhaps a short story for a child you know. A free piece of writing, a gift, that will bring them unexpected joy. Then go and put it in the post box and know you did a good thing today.

JULY

# 16th July

*"The writer is by nature a dreamer – a conscious dreamer."*
Carson McCullers

An evocative quote, isn't it? Today's task is to use this as a first line in a story or scene. Where do you go from here? What does it mean to *consciously* dream?

# 17th July

*"And so with the sunshine and the great bursts of leaves
growing on the trees, just as things grow in fast movies,
I had that familiar conviction that life was beginning over
again with the summer."*
F. Scott Fitzgerald, *The Great Gatsby*

Here, F. Scott Fitzgerald captures the energy of summer, the nearly pulsating nature of the plants expanding as they reach for the sunshine. He almost personifies them. Today, your task is to choose a plant. Anything, from a pot plant in your room to a Venus flytrap. Now draw it – feel free to use the internet to find the details of its appearance. Pay attention to its colour, texture, scale. Have a *really* good look at it.

Now write a list of the plant's characteristics and begin to personify it. Every word on your list should be applicable to both the plant and a person. Is it wiry, spry, spindly or blooming? Does it seem warm and inviting, or sharp and sinister?

This list will become your character description. Now, here's the challenge. Write a scenario in which this character appears (as a person). In your scene, this character must be active. They must do something to change the course of the scene, meaning we end the scene in different circumstances, to give it drama. Write it fully, enjoy getting to know your protagonist.

Here's where it gets *very* interesting. Rethink your scene, but replace the person with the plant. How do you make the story work now? Why not write in the first person *as* the plant? Try it, even if it seems unusual; it could be the most inventive thing you've ever written. Anything can be a character. Keep your mind open when you're writing. It always pays off. I mean, *Little Shop of Horrors* was one of the most successful musicals of the twentieth century, and who was its star? Audrey II, the carnivorous plant.

# 18th July

*"Fantasy is hardly an escape from reality.
It's a way of understanding it."*
Lloyd Alexander

'Once upon a time…' The most overused story beginning out there. Well, today we're going to have a bit of fun with that.

Write 'Once upon a time' thirty times in your notebook. Go on, crack on with it – I know you're cursing me right now but I can take it. Now set your timer for eight minutes. Your task is to write thirty opening lines for thrilling books, each beginning 'Once upon a time'. That's only sixteen seconds to write each starting sentence.

Play around with your responses. Make them very long, very short, wry, serious, romantic, obtuse, verbose, ridiculunks using made-up words. Go wild. Then afterwards, if any of them take your fancy, go ahead and write what happens next.

# 19th July

*"Good writers define reality; bad ones merely restate it.
A good writer turns fact into truth; a bad writer will,
more often than not, accomplish the opposite."*
Edward Albee

Today is a simple writing-prompt day – and your task is to write about:

*Having to tell someone the truth.*

Make it up if you would rather, but if you do choose to write from a personal perspective, be as honest as you can. It's a worthy life skill.

# 20th July

*"You never have to change anything
you got up in the middle of the night to write."*
Saul Bellow

Today is **Moon Day**. There's such a romantic association with the moon, and the myths and magic that accompany it. There's also a lot of scientific evidence that the moon changes our behaviour – whether because of gravitational pull or simply the fact that a full moon means more light, which can mean everything from sleeplessness and more babies being born to more car crashes. So, to celebrate the power of night and the moon, you need to wait till nightfall to do today's task.

Leave it until as late at night as you can, find a calm and quiet place, then take a look at the moon, at space, at the breadth of the sky. How does it make you feel? Then you're going to journal (free-write). Journalling before bed calms your brain and quells anxiety. It is also when a lot of people have their best ideas. When you're ready, set a (gentle!) alarm and begin. Write for ten minutes.

...or all night, if you so desire. Just don't go out and crash your car.

# 21st July

*"Never compete with living writers. You don't know whether they're good or not. Compete with the dead ones you know are good. Then when you can pass them up you know you're going good. You should have read all the good stuff so that you know what has been done, because if you have a story like one somebody else has written, yours isn't any good unless you can write a better one. In any art you're allowed to steal anything if you can make it better, but the tendency should always be upward instead of down. And don't ever imitate anybody."*
Ernest Hemingway

Today, in honour of the great **Ernest Hemingway** on his birthday, we're going to do his exercise for 'Sharpening Observation Skills'. So go grab a notebook and head out, imagining that you're an artist heading out with an easel or sketchbook to capture what you see and feel. The artist's job is to pay *very* close attention to everything that's going on, both externally and the internal impact – how does what you see make you feel? Hemingway was a great believer in specificity and detail.

Find a spot. Sit and observe *everything*. Watch what happens. Be detailed in your observations. Write it all down. Take in any sound, any dialogue, the aural landscape in its entirety. Observe your emotions, and what *exactly* gives you these feelings. Is it a flash of colour on a skirt, a comment you overhear, a noise as someone skids on their bike? What does it do to you, physically, emotionally? Record this in detail. Your reader must be able to understand the reason you felt something and what it felt like, so they can imagine it too.

Hemingway's philosophy was never to be vague. 'Don't just tell us catching a fish is exciting. Be specific. Show us why.'

# 22nd July

*"People who work hard often work too hard...*
*May we learn to honor the hammock, the siesta, the nap and*
*the pause in all its forms."*
Alice Walker

Today is **International Hammock Day**. Hurrah! Holiday!

So you know what...? Today, have a rest! Have a day off and go and enjoy yourself. Use your writing time to do something delightfully enjoyable. *Not* chores. Not work. Something for you.

And if you are *determined* to write something, imagine you're lying in a hammock. What can you see, where are you, and what are you doing? And write in a spirit of calm. I mean, you could even pour yourself a cocktail...

JULY

239

# 23rd July

*"Summer afternoon – to me those have always been the two most beautiful words in the English language."*
Henry James, *The Portrait of a Lady*

What better to do on a sunny summer afternoon than relax with a good book? Bliss. So, a little anecdote for you. I had a realisation recently, as my bookshelves began to sag and I tried desperately to find space for the *new* novels I kept buying... and ignored the piles of old books that I was avoiding reading. You know, the books you feel you *ought* to read, or unwanted presents, or the book you think 'I *should* read it, everyone else has, even though it's four thousand pages of tiny print and printed on crêpe paper'? Yup. Those books I conveniently ignored in favour of the new 'most talked about' publication that everyone is gassing about?

So I made a resolution. For every new book I read, I would read one from my shelf of doom. I put them in titular alphabetical order, so I wouldn't have any choice about which was next, in order to avoid still self-selecting the most appealing (shortest) ones.

And I began. And what was up first? Dammit! Only one of the reputedly most harrowing books of the twentieth century, a tome at 814 pages (which is rude, right? I have stuff to do). The book was *A Little Life* by Hanya Yanagihara. And no joke: it was one of the best books I have ever read. EVER. I couldn't put it down. I mourned for it after I'd finished it. And, dear reader, it won't surprise you to know that that shelf was FULL. OF. FRICKING. GEMS.

Your task today is to pull out a novel that you have been avoiding reading, go somewhere quiet and give this book the respect to read the first twenty-five pages. No excuses. I'll bet you get hooked.

And if it's rubbish, after twenty-five pages you have my full permission to give it Oxfam.

# 24th July

Today we're going to focus on capturing the feeling of summer, but avoiding the much-trodden path of 'classical summer scenes' – the boating lakes, the straw hats, the young beautiful people in white linen running through fields of long grass.

Your task is to choose a location that says 'summer' to you. Write from your real experience. To me, the epitome of summer is the melee of colour and noise that is Brockwell Lido in a heatwave. Between vibrant, bustling Brixton and leafy Herne Hill, the lido sits on the edge of Brockwell Park and quickly becomes the hub where South London turns out to cool off, sunbathe and avoid work on the terrace of the 1930s pool. It is *heaving*. With crowds of young Colombians with basketballs and picnics, Caribbean families with great-grandmas and great-grandchildren sharing platters of home-made grub, all shoved up next to 'yummy mummies' from rarefied Dulwich with their competitive pushchairs and kids scavenging for slices of pizza. And the pool itself, slick with an oil skin of suncream, dive-bombed by teenagers as toddlers take their first dips, and the serious swimmers still persist in getting their kilometres in. It's a place of wonder, chaos, teenage dreams, family sagas, and joy. And to me, it is summer.

What's summer to you?

# 25th July

*"The truth will set you free. But first, it will piss you off."*
Gloria Steinem

Today is a simple writing-prompt day. Inspired by one of my absolute heroes, let's do a task for Gloria. I want you to write about:

*A time you wish you'd done something differently.*

Write it first with the situation as it really played out. Then write the scenario again, but this time with an alternative outcome.

# 26th July

*"My method is to take the utmost trouble to find the right thing to say, and then to say it with the utmost levity."*
George Bernard Shaw

**George Bernard Shaw,** born on this day, was a lover of words. I mean, some (me) would say he often used too many of them. But hey, he didn't do too badly for himself.

He had a truly distinctive voice, something that many new writers struggle to find – defining your tone, your attitude, your vocabulary. So today's task gives you an opportunity to think about voice and style, and work out the tone you gravitate towards writing in.

Pick a book at random and select a paragraph. Now, rewrite it in the following styles:

1. *Florid*: As descriptively as possibly, using elevated vocabulary and as much added detail as you can muster.

2. *Sensual*: Rewrite it making full use of all five senses. Note that this is different from florid – it's about making your prose experiential.

3. *Sparsely*: Take out everything you don't think is necessary. Cut it to its bare minimum. Be brutal with those scissors.

4. *Stylistically*: Think of a writer you like and mimic their style. Do they use a particular sentence structure, tone, type of vocabulary? What give their voice character?

5. *Culturally*: Often the most specific voices give us a sense of the writer's cultural background, an accent, a heritage of language – both in choice of words and syntax. Try it. Using your own cultural dialect if you have one. And if not, one you are familiar with.

6. *Your way*: Whatever this is. Have a go.

# 27th July

*"A novel worth reading is an education of the heart.*
*It enlarges your sense of human possibility,*
*of what human nature is, of what happens in the world.*
*It's a creator of inwardness."*
Susan Sontag

Susan Sontag was a brilliant essayist and thinker. Whilst she had many a good thing to say about reading, she is perhaps best known for her philosophies on photography. Have a read of her aptly named *On Photography* if you're interested, it's a fascinating deep-dive into images, why we record them and how we read them.

Today's task is a visual one. Take a camera and go for a walk. Take ten photographs that, between them, tell a story. It may be linear. It might be quite abstract, but – for our purpose as storytellers – try to find a sense of shape, a beginning, middle and end of some sort. There are two ways to approach this task. Either, you could give yourself time to spend in an area and just take it in. Then, when you have gathered thoughts and interesting subjects, you could take your photos in order to tell a story.

Or you can do the 'my mother at a jumble sale' approach. That is to say, turn up and grab *everything*. Take loads of photos – all things you find interesting – then stagger home with them and look at them all, constructing your story after the event.

However you do it, put ten still images together in a series that tells a story. Look at that – a pictorial tale! It's good to find your inspiration in places that you don't expect. And we, as writers, have to get used to looking and observing as much as possible. Be curious, as Sontag herself said:

*'Do stuff. Be clenched, curious. Not waiting for inspiration's shove or society's kiss on your forehead. Pay attention. It's all about paying attention. Attention is vitality. It connects you with others. It makes you eager. Stay eager.'*

# 28th July

Beatrix Potter was a prolific writer, yet first and foremost she was an artist and naturalist – and took her studies *very* seriously. She kept hundreds of notebooks of animal sketches, detailed journals and research notes, making an effort to expand her knowledge of animals on a daily basis. Her characters were born out of this rigorous research.

Today, on **Beatrix Potter's birthday,** pick a topic that excites you. Spend at least half an hour researching it. You're looking for a potential character in amongst the facts. For example, if you're interested in mountaineering, read articles about famous expeditions, some contemporary, others historical. Are you more intrigued by the Victorian mountaineers' amusing means of staying warm before modern technology? Or is there a dramatic modern story that tempts you to read on, because you can relate to it? Or are you more interested in mystery? You might read about the Dyatlov Pass incident, for example, in which a group of Russian students went missing in the oddest of circumstances, a mystery that has never been solved.

From your research, pin down a person you want to focus on. Perhaps they're real, like Fanny Bullock Workman, the first woman we know of to climb the Himalayas. Or perhaps you might get an idea for a fictional character – did Fanny meet a Sherpa who helped her? Who was that, and what was their relationship?

When you have your character, draw them in detail. Then write them a short story, through which you will get to know them. If you like them, put them in your mental 'character bank' and perhaps they will become a protagonist in a fully fledged story you'll write on another day – maybe even on a mountaineering trip.

# 29th July

*"We should all be feminists."*
Chimamanda Ngozi Adichie

On this day in 2014, Adichie published her game-changing book, *We Should All Be Feminists*. If you haven't read it, do it. It's both short and excellent.

Today's task is to write a passage with a female protagonist in a role you would never expect to see them in. It can be set at any point in history, the past or future. It can be as wild or as realistic as you like. And it doesn't need to be heroic. Yes, you could write about the first woman to... ride in a hot-air balloon, fly a fighter plane, become a university professor, be ordained as a rabbi, to officiate a football match... But you could also write about women whose roles are far more conventional, even domestic, and what small incidents they encounter that have an emotional impact on them, even if they have no effect on the outside world. As George Eliot so astutely commented in *Middlemarch*:

> 'the growing good of the world is partly dependent on unhistoric acts; and that things are not so ill with you and me as they might have been, is half owing to the number who lived faithfully a hidden life, and rest in unvisited tombs.'

Consider how open this task is, and all the possibilities of what a 'woman's role' can mean, for good or bad. You don't have to write about heroines; naughty women are often more exciting!

# 30th July

*"To understand is to perceive patterns."*
Isaiah Berlin

Let's talk about motifs: recurring images that expand on a theme and illuminate an idea. A butterfly in the hedge at a picnic, whose fate is somehow paralleled with the action of the scene. Sometimes directly in parallel, sometimes the opposite – the butterfly might fly to freedom just as we understand our characters are truly trapped by their own situation. The poignancy of this juxtaposition adds to the emotional impact of the scene and layers nuance and depth into the writing. If you were writing that scene, you would track the butterfly at several points during the scene, in order that this motif adds to the drama.

Pick a theme. To be trapped, for example. Perhaps your theme might be hope, or connection, or the unfairness of fate… choose something that has an emotional core. Then pick an appropriate scenario or location.

Now choose something symbolic that can mirror the main action. Your task is to utilise this motif, weaving in and out of the drama, through which you increase the emotional weight of your scene.

# 31st July

*"If a story is in you, it has to come out."*
William Faulkner

Some writers have magnificent studies. Luxurious desks. A chaise longue to ponder on while they dream up their next masterpiece. If that's you – lucky you! Can I come and work at yours, please?

Most of us aren't that lucky – and don't spend that much time at home. So here's a simple truth for you. If you want to get anywhere as a writer, or any sort of creative, you have to learn to work everywhere. Don't have an office? Or a desk? Or time? Do it anyway. Learn that fifteen minutes on a bus might be the golden time when you invent your best-ever plot twist. I write so frequently on public transport that, if you are a Londoner, you may well have seen me sitting at a bus stop or going round the Circle Line on loop because I just got into an idea and I need to get it scribbled down before it flits back into the ether.

And the same applies to time. Rather than fixating on creating an effective routine, realise that you can spin ideas in the gaps between other tasks. So today's challenge is to write in all the gaps. Begin a writing task in the morning and carry it around with you. It can be anything you want – a short story, a poem, a scene. If you need inspiration, flick through this book and find a prompt you haven't used yet. And whenever you have a gap, when you would normally get out your phone, or have a nap – write instead. See what you achieve by the end of the day. You might surprise yourself.

JULY

# August

# 1st August

*"Without leaps of imagination or dreaming,
we lose the excitement of possibilities.
Dreaming, after all is a form of planning."*
Gloria Steinem

Today it's **International Planner Day**. Apparently. Personally, I am not a fan of planning. No plan fan, I. Screenwriters are always being asked for 'treatments' and 'beat sheets' that outline what is going to happen in a plot. To which my response is: 'Please no!' How do I know how characters will behave before I've spent time with them? I can only work out what a character is going to do – and, crucially, how they might surprise me – by spending time writing in their voice. It's like hanging out with them. Without a voice, dialogue, they're simply a two-dimensional cut-out. Anything that I can work out in a two-page 'plan' won't have the benefit of that time spent in their world; that's when, to me, they become real and fleshy, contradictory, complex and challenging, when they start to surprise me. And that's the magic.

So even though it's planning day, we're not going to use today to plan a piece of work. Instead, we're going to do some dream planning. A whimsical, no-commitment, imaginative list of what you *might* like to do as a writer over the next few months. Write a list of ten things (minimum) that you'd like to write. Don't overthink it – just start. And the more specific, the better. 'I'd like to write a short story in the voice of a supermarket self-checkout.' 'I'd like to write something about my grandmother.' 'I'd like to write something dark, set on The High Line in Manhattan involving a creepy teenager, a glowing lemon squeezer and a strange bush.' Anything. Just make the list. And if an idea sparks… you could even start writing!

# 2nd August

Today is **National Colouring Book Day**. Colour can be a great tool for writers, not only in describing what something looks like, but to create tone and emotion. But it's also the easiest place to fall into the cliché trap. 'He was green with envy.' 'Her mood was black.' No thank you – we can do better than that.

Write a short passage describing an emotional event. But instead of using the normal senses and emotional words, use colour instead. But no 'anger is red, sadness is blue' predictability please – stop right there! Your task is to use a colour palette that is *not* what we'd expect, but somehow feels true. Perhaps a growing feeling of sadness might be a bright, overwhelming purple. Perhaps happiness is black because it feels like space and liberty. Perhaps jealousy is a hot, searing yellow. Have a go. It might surprise you.

# 3rd August

*"Discipline is important, but so is taking a breath and looking around, and giving things a chance to germinate."*
Madeline Miller

Lots of folks say the most important tool for a writer is life experience. So today, instead of writing, do.

Do something that expands your life experience by going somewhere out of character. It doesn't have to be crazily out of your comfort zone. You don't have to do a bungee jump. Make a list of places and activities within your natural territory... and get out of it. Pick the opposite. Recently I took my boyfriend for a facial. He didn't know what to do with himself, it was *so* outside his usual experience. Okay, I'll be honest, I don't think he'd go again, but, if he ever wanted to, he'd be far better tooled now to write from the perspective of the kind of person with a penchant for the occasional spa trip. Which is, frankly, a lot of us.

So, if you generally shop at organic farmers' markets, go to a cheap chicken shop and have a kebab. Sit inside and watch the goings-on. Who else is in there? What's the chat? What details can you observe? If you are a regular charity shopper, go to Selfridges and *pretend* you might buy something. Go to a swanky hotel, order a cocktail and sit at the bar. Go somewhere you normally walk past. A laundrette. Penny arcade. Casino. Go to a gig. A museum. Whatever doesn't normally float your boat. And hang out. Take it in. Enjoy. This is life experience! You never know, maybe you'll fall in love with this new world. Just don't blame me if you become a gambling addict.

You don't have to write about it later, but if you want to – do, from the perspective of one of the people you saw.

# 4th August

*"One of the things that happens when you write characters –
and maybe this is my own sentimentality – is that I always
find I have an instinct to protect them."*
Greta Gerwig

Film-maker **Greta Gerwig**, born on this day, kicked off her career writing screenplays about a young woman negotiating her way through the world. Always unapologetically biographical, it meant there was an authenticity and honesty in her work, which is partly why it has become so popular.

Today's task is to write a dialogue scene dramatising a moment in your own teenage years. Consider the best entry point into your scene – and the best place to jump out; usually the later you get into and the earlier you get out of the drama, the better. Drop us into the action mid-scene. Pull us out as we're still wanting more, leaving an element of mystery – there's nothing more thrilling than a scene that ends on a cliffhanger.

Think about your characters. Make sure their voices are distinct – i.e. their dialogue is personally specific. You should be able to tell which character is talking if you take the names away, simply from the way they speak.

Try to write the scene as accurately as possible from memory, then edit it to make it more cinematic and dramatic. Truth is now disposable. Drama is king.

# 5th August

*"The idea that I'm going to have to sit down to write some fiction where I'm going to have to think of a plot would really scare me, because it would come out a mess."*
Tracey Emin

Oh, plotting. Thinking of a story is hard! So let's break it down and focus on structure, from which you can build plot.

All we need at this stage are four, simple ingredients:

1. *The Set-up* – where we establish the world as it is before the story changes everything.

2. *The Dilemma* – a catalyst that turns the world of the set-up upside down and challenges our protagonist.

3. *The Journey* – the attempt to solve the dilemma and the path that it takes our hero on.

4. *The Ending* – the solution, in which the story 'pays off' and we have a sense that all ends are tied up, questions are answered and the journey is complete.

Here's a secret for you. It's much easier to think of a good dilemma than it is an exciting set-up. A set-up is just 'the world as it is' *before* the drama… not so interesting. Dilemmas are cool. It's a girl in a Muslim country who wants to ride a bicycle like her brothers, but isn't allowed to in public. How is she going to get one… and get away with it? (See the sensational film *Wadjda*.) It's the woman who marries the man of her dreams, only to find out that the spectre of his ex-wife is haunting them – what is she going to do about it? (Du Maurier's *Rebecca*.)

So now come up with five dilemmas, each a problem for a protagonist. Here's a hint: whatever sort of person your protagonist is, make the problem something that challenges the essence of who they are.

A man terrified of heights who has to climb a mountain to rescue his child. The pacifist who has to learn to fight. The kid who's never been left home alone who suddenly has to defend his house from burglars.

When you have your five dilemmas, now write the set-ups for each – the world before the dilemma (i.e. the status quo, the peaceful world, where 'everything is normal'). Here's a tip: the more the world in the set-up is the antithesis of the dilemma, the better the drama. Make it as hard for your protagonists as possible. The more the kid left home alone was overprotected by his fussing parents, the more valuables there are to steal in the house, the more clueless he is about how to be 'home alone'…

Then, you guessed it, outline the journey. You're going to write a *very brief* overview of the journey they go on… and how it is resolved at the end. Try to give the journey an arc, with at least one major high and major low.

Finally, create a good, dramatic ending, which means your protagonist is fundamentally changed by the action of the story. The miser becomes generous (Scrooge). The bullied orphan becomes the best wizard ever (guess who…).

There you go. You now have five plots. Well done! Now sell them to Hollywood, become a millionaire and send me a cheque in the post.

# 6th August

Yesterday you came up with a series of plot scenarios. So today,
inspired by **Lord Tennyson,** whose birthday is today, let's master
those passions!

You're going to pick a scene from one of your five scenarios and
write it. If you're not sure which to choose, I'd pick a dilemma scene
as there's bound to be a big juicy bit of drama where the 'problem'
explodes into the protagonist's life. Feel free to write this as prose or
dialogue – just make it dramatic.

If you didn't do yesterday's exercise, guess what – now's a great time
to catch up!

# 7th August

*"Everything begins with an idea."*
Earl Nightingale

Today we're going to play *Word Salad*.

Set a timer for twenty minutes. Your task is to write without stopping – anything you like – but the challenge is you have to use at least five of these words and phrases, in any order… the more, the better! An extra point for each word. Ready – go!

Newt, bandage, corner shop, mellifluous, east, urge, bread bin, flash, ocular, wind chime, Zambia, cottage, frenetic, pond, space–time continuum, master, beat, broccoli, riffing, spectacular, face-off, piecemeal, fraying, whisk, bollocks, sundried, paw, headband, scratchy, pumpkin, fret, folio, jingle.

# 8th August

*"Methinks that the moment my legs begin to move
my thoughts begin to flow."*
Henry David Thoreau

It's August. Hopefully the weather is nice (if you're in certain parts of the world) – so let's get outside and take some inspiration from one of the most mindful, creatively sparking activities… walking. Charles Dickens apparently walked twenty to thirty miles a day, formulating his characters and composing dialogue, which he would then write up when he got home. So there you go. A couple of times round the block shouldn't be hard.

Go out and walk for at least ten minutes, taking in everything, using all five senses. Then, when you find an appropriate perch, take out your notebook, set your timer and free-write for ten minutes. Write without stopping, don't censor yourself, and write down everything that you see, hear, smell, experience. Any bits of dialogue you overhear. Anything you notice, observe or imagine is happening in an interaction if you're in a street; if you're out in nature, watch for the minutiae of the physical world around you.

Walk home. Now look at your writing and pick your favourite lines. Edit it into something interesting. Perhaps it'll end up just a single sentence. Perhaps it will become a novel!

# 9th August

*"A writer is, after all, only half his book. The other half is the reader and from the reader the writer learns."*
P. L. Travers

**P. L. Travers** – born on this day – was the rather cantankerous genius who created the magical nanny Mary Poppins. Interesting that the book is so full of joy and delight when she herself… wasn't. She wrote *for her readers*.

Have a think about your motivation for writing. Do you want to entertain, to move, to teach, to thrill? If you can work that out, it will help steer you towards what you really want to write. I like to conjure magic if I can: to provide an escape, to make people laugh, to have my readers feel something deeply. I like to say something that is worthwhile. To make people think. To leave an audience feeling a little bit better and more inspired about the world than they were at the beginning. Lord, no wonder it's so hard to write something I like!

But that all tells me what sort of writer I want to be, and what I want to write about. I like writing comedy with heart, about underdogs, about people who wouldn't normally be in the limelight, unlikely heroes – big hearts and big feelings. So I'm not about to embark on writing a noir thriller. This saves me loads of time – I'm pretty focused on what I choose to write, and if I'm given the opportunity to pitch for a heart-wrenching state-of-the-nation political saga, I know it's not for me.

Your task today is to write a letter to your readers, telling them what you want them to get from your writing. Hopefully this will help you focus your own aims and start thinking clearly about what you might write next.

# 10th August

Today – on **National Lazy Day** – you have my permission to do nothing. Okay, not *quite* nothing. All I want you to do is daydream. Because, you know what… daydreaming, letting your mind roll into subconscious mode, is often where we have our most creative ideas. When your brain isn't trying to be active, when you're just moseying around in the backwaters of your subconscious, that's often when the most original thoughts arrive.

Set a timer for ten minutes, find a comfortable chair, close your eyes and spend the ten minutes daydreaming. See where you go. Just try not to fall asleep!

AUGUST

# 11th August

*"The best way to treat obstacles is to use them as stepping stones. Laugh at them, tread on them, and let them lead you to something better."*
Enid Blyton

The creator of so many beloved characters – the Famous Five, the Secret Seven, the Magic Faraway Tree's inhabitants, Noddy – **Enid Blyton** certainly was prolific – and today was her birthday. Read her suggestions, then do as she says and write something today. It can be anything. But write *something*.

1. Write every day – Even if you have nothing to say – write *something* every day. Perhaps it isn't prose, you might just journal, write a blog, a haiku – but write.

2. Write what you know – This might seem ironic when lots of Blyton's scenarios were fantastical, but she was hugely committed to writing from observations of life, incorporating elements of reality. Use your own experience as a basis for your work – that'll ensure it's always authentic.

3. Don't give up – Like most aspiring writers, Blyton was rejected *a lot*. But she persevered, kept on writing, kept on sending manuscripts, until she hit the jackpot. Keep on keeping on.

4. Keep in touch with your audience – Blyton received huge amounts of fan mail, and incredibly she replied to most of it. She valued hearing what her readers liked, what they wanted, what had struck a chord. I don't believe you should ever write exclusively to please an audience – you have to write for yourself if you are going to stay original and authentic – but it's useful to have a sense of who you are writing for, and to stay in touch with their experience of the world in order to capture it in your writing.

# 12th August

*"My record collection probably tells the story of my life better than I could in words."*
Colleen Murphy

One form of writing we don't talk about much is songwriting, partially because it's *hard*! Lyrics are as complicated to write, and get right, as any other form. So, because it's **Vinyl Record Day** today, take a beat – no pun intended – to appreciate the art of songwriting, and the inspiration that music can be.

Pick four contrasting songs from your music collection that you think are interesting lyrically. Now settle down and listen with open ears. How does each tell a story? How do they use language to do that? Who is the character that's singing? Which of your four songs affects you most lyrically? And would it still if you take the music away? Plenty of songwriters are brilliant poets – Leonard Cohen, Joni Mitchell, Dolly Parton, Taylor Swift, Beyoncé, Lizzo – with such distinctive narrative voices, making specific choices in terms of vocabulary and poetic form. Sit back, relax and enjoy. Perhaps soon you might feel inspired to write a song yourself.

AUGUST

# 13th August

*"Drama is life with the dull bits cut out."*
Alfred Hitchcock

Happy birthday, **Alfred Hitchcock**! To celebrate the main man, pick one of the following lines – each from a different Hitchcock film – as a writing prompt for today:

1. I'm a bit rattled tonight. You see, I happen at this moment to be dead. (*The 39 Steps*)

2. Intelligence. Nothing has caused the human race so much trouble as intelligence. (*Rear Window*)

3. A boy's best friend is his mother. (*Psycho*)

# 14th August

*"My spelling is Wobbly. It's good spelling but it Wobbles, and the letters get in the wrong places."*
A. A. Milne, *Winnie-the-Pooh*

Let's talk about editing. It isn't just correcting spelling mistakes, far from it. An editor's job is to look for potential cuts, improvements, opportunities to expand an idea, to clarify: 'How do you make this work better?' Editors are an essential part of the process when bringing a story to life.

For today's task, pick a paragraph from a book at random, write it out, then set to task as an editor. Using a coloured pen, notate it, working out how you think it could be improved. Sometimes it's hard to look at your own work with perspective, so practise by trying it on someone else's. Just don't bother with editing John Steinbeck, cos every line is perfect.*

* Disclaimer: All opinions are my own and are also 100% fact.

# 15th August

*"The sprouting of the seeds of creativity,
intuition and wisdom takes place in a relaxed mind.
Only anger, greed and ego require a disturbed mind."*
Shivanshu K. Srivastava

Today is **National Relaxation Day**! So here's a lovely gentle exercise that has, at its heart, that daydreamy feeling that you get when you're lying around.

You're going to do a piece of stream-of-consciousness writing. Take some paper and a pen. Set a timer. Now write for five minutes without taking your pen off the paper. You must write constantly. When you get stuck for what to write, write the word 'rubbish' over and over until you work out how to carry on. Do this until the timer goes off.

Sounds odd. But just see what comes out. It may be a rant about this being pointless. It may be a list of everything you can see, or thoughts that pop into your head. It may become a story. You may end up writing on a random theme. But trust in seeing what happens rather than deciding in advance. I like the challenge of starting with nothing and seeing where you end up.

Now, usually I'd insist you do more with it. But guess what – today is National Relaxation Day, so what the hell, that's enough! This sort of spontaneous writing is a worthwhile act of creativity in itself. Some folks do this every morning – it's the idea of 'morning pages' from *The Artist's Way* by Julia Cameron. She sees it as a creativity kick-starter. It's good training. And it makes you realise that writing is about getting on with it. It's a muscle that you're exercising. And that's enough.

However, if that's now got your creative bubbles popping, let's carry on, as follows:

Take this five-minute splurge writing as your research. Your brain dump. It's what poured out, unedited. So now – let's do something with it.

First, re-read it and underline any bits you like. Write them out separately as a new piece. Now edit, edit, edit. What's good, what fits together. Feel free to add to it, expand it. Look at your choice of vocabulary – can you make it more interesting? These lines are no longer sacred – they are merely a jumping-off point – so edit as you wish.

Now, once you've got lines you are more pleased with, put them together into something new. A short paragraph. A stanza of a poem. Whatever you fancy. It can be super-short, two lines even – but it'll be interesting.

There you go – National Relaxation Day and you've already achieved something. So now you really can just flop on the sofa and binge-watch Netflix for the whole day with no guilt.

Sometimes the best writing comes from something that was buried somewhere in our subconscious, that you can only tempt out by forcing yourself to write without self-censoring. That's what's great about stream of consciousness. It often feels painful, but that's because it's *good for you*. Like cod liver oil. Or going to the gym. Think long-term gains. And try to enjoy it. Who knows – maybe you'll start doing 'morning pages' every day...

# 16th August

*"All good comedy comes from a place of anger.
Figure out what's making you angry and work on it from there."*
Jerry Seinfeld

It's **Tell a Joke Day**. One way to find comedy in a scenario is to look at it from the perspective of the comic outsider. A scene of marital break-up would normally read as very serious… unless it's viewed through the window by a nosy granny who is passing by, delighting in what she sees, feeling like she's lucked out with tonight's excellent show. The more she relishes the tears and distress, the funnier the scene will be.

Pick a serious scenario, either from a book or film, or one that you conjure up yourself (avoid anything brutal or harrowing).

Now pick an outsider who might be on the edge of the scene. They shouldn't get involved; they are simply noticing it from a distance. It could be a child watching adults, a street cleaner observing drama on the high road, a supermarket worker witnessing a major event. The more dramatic the scene, and the more your outsider misunderstands or lacks empathy with it, the funnier it can be.

Scout and Jem in *To Kill a Mockingbird* are prime examples of outside witnesses to a bigger drama, particularly as they are too young to fully understand what they are witnessing. L. P. Hartley's *The Go-Between* also plays this game, and it works brilliantly in terms of upping the tension and drama. In both these instances (neither comic, I'll admit), the observers eventually get involved. How could they not get intwined in the drama?!

# 17th August

*"The creatures outside looked from pig to man,
and from man to pig, and from pig to man again;
but already it was impossible to say which was which."*
George Orwell, *Animal Farm*

On this day in 1945, George Orwell's revolutionary satire *Animal Farm* was published. The story is an allegory for the history of Soviet Communism. By choosing a farm setting and recasting the politicians as animals, he creates a fable to disguise (somewhat) his message.

Your task today is to write a short fable. Pick an issue you care deeply about and think of the most important message or lesson that compounds it. Issues of inequality, justice and fairness are good places to start.

Now choose a completely contrasting setting in which to tell your story. Remove from it the realm of reality, people and the modern day – and place it somewhere else, as Orwell did. See if you can tell a story that conveys your message without ever having to talk politics explicitly.

# 18th August

*"It takes a lot of bad writing to get to a little good writing."*
Truman Capote

Today is **Bad Poetry Day**, so your task is to write the worst possible poem. Think of all the clichés that make poems 'bad'. Bad rhymes, trying too hard, fake romance, overused clichés, boring words, saccharine sentiments, terrible metaphors, lack of sense. Go to town on making it horrendous – and enjoy every moment.

You never know, you might accidentally write something brilliant! Carol Ann Duffy's poem 'Valentine' sounds, if you were to describe it to an outsider, like it might be awful... she compares her love to an onion. But of course, it is Duffy, so it is quite, quite brilliant.

# 19th August

*"The best thing about a picture is that it never changes, even when the people in it do."*
Andy Warhol

Today, think about character – but don't write anything. Instead, sketch a character – without planning them. Just draw spontaneously, and as you do, add as much detail as you can. Who are they? What are they wearing, what are they carrying, what is their demeanour, what are they doing?

Repeat three times – you now have three spontaneously created people, ready to go. Give them names and keep them in your back pocket, ready to spring out the next time you need a character for a story. Or simply save them for tomorrow – when they're going to come in very handy…

# 20th August

*"The second draft is on yellow paper, that's when I work on characterizations. The third is pink, I work on story motivations. Then blue, that's where I cut, cut, cut."*
Jacqueline Susann

There are many layers when you're creating a character-driven story. Building your protagonists, piece by piece, getting to know them, working out who they are.

Today you are going to take the three characters you drew yesterday and put them in a scenario together. And write the scene. Let's get to know these three people and work out what their relationships might be. It's by trying your characters out in different places, getting them to talk to different people, challenging them, that you will get to know them and to start to form their voice. They become active. And action is essential to plot.

# 21st August

*"Summertime is always the best of what might be."*
Charles Bowden

When I was growing up, the last couple of weeks of August always started to feel like the end of the summer delights. The roll towards term starting again, when you wanted to milk every last moment for the chance to stay out as late as possible until the last remnants of sun disappeared.

So, with that in mind, use today for a bit of reflection. As the year is rolling on, ask yourself, as a writer, what have you achieved? What have you written that you like? That you don't like? What forms of writing are starting to float your boat? What do you most enjoy? What sort of exercises have provoked useful ideas? And thinking ahead, what would you like to achieve between now and the end of the year? What do you dream of writing? Is there something you are really craving as a storyteller?

Write down your aims and pin them somewhere you can see them, as motivation.

# 22nd August

*"I hate writing, I love having written."*
Dorothy Parker

**Dorothy Parker,** born today, was a wit and a brilliant poet. Her poem 'One Perfect Rose' is a hilarious yet carefully observed revisionist take on a flower poem, to quote a little of it:

> *'Why is it no one ever sent me yet*
> *One perfect limousine, do you suppose?*
> *Ah no, it's always just my luck to get*
> *One perfect rose.'*

Look it up and read the whole thing. Your task today is to write the scene that inspired this poem, between our witty protagonist and her lover. See if you can channel her voice, her wry wit. Have fun!

# 23rd August

*"An animal's eyes have the power to speak a great language."*
Martin Buber

Today's exercise is inspired by the fact that my dog, Newt – a very licky Cocker Spaniel – is staring at me, watching me work. I *think* he thinks I might have a treat for him, but who knows what he's really thinking?

So today your task is to write a dramatic scene, but through the eyes and experience of a pet. Is it a nonchalant cat who has seen it all before? Or an emotionally invested dog who can't bear to see his owners argue? What interesting scenario would lend itself most dramatically to this form? Does the pet observe something they shouldn't have? Do they need to alert someone? Who might bribe them to keep schtum? Or might this wily pet have its own agenda?

# 24th August

*"What literature can and should do is change the people who teach the people who don't read the books."*
A. S. Byatt

Choose a protagonist. Someone you know, that you've seen, a character you've been writing. Next, pick the three people that your character is least likely to have dinner with.

And now… write the scene!

# 25th August

"When I create music, the feeling that you get... I get
first. You [the listener] have a delayed experience with the
feeling I initially get when I have a creative insight... There is
a high. There is an emotional experience that happens when
everything comes together... I made music as consistently as
I did; especially back in the day, because it made me feel so
good... When everything is on, it's a wonderful feeling."
Lauryn Hill

Lauryn Hill was a goddess to me when I was a teenager. A bold,
headstrong, say-it-like-it-is woman whose music was the soundtrack
to all of my teenage dramas, dating disasters and late-night soul-
searching (with a healthy accompaniment of cheese and ketchup on
toast). Her incredible album *The Miseducation of Lauryn Hill* was
released on this day in 1998.

One stand-out element of her writing is her specificity in conjuring
the world that she grew up in. Take a look at the lyrics of 'Every
Ghetto, Every City', and note the details – the locations ('*Springfield
Avenue had the best popsicles*'), what they're eating ('*a beef patty and
some coco bread*'), who her friends are and what they're wearing
('*Freyling-Huysen used to have the bomb leather*'), what they're chatting
about, who's dating who and what their youthful attitude to life is
('*Back then we thought we'd all live forever*').

These lyrics immerse us immediately in her world. Your task today
is to write some verses that capture your teenage years. Lauryn's are
brilliant partly because they're not about life-changing incidents,
they're about everyday life. She makes us realise how much colour
and interest there is in a 'normal' day, when you make detailed
enough observations.

You can either write your lyrics in the form of a poem, or choose
a song and try to copy the scansion as an outline for yours.

# 26th August

*"I've got the key to my castle in the air,
but whether I can unlock the door remains to be seen."*
Louisa May Alcott, *Little Women*

Louisa May Alcott is best known for her book *Little Women*, and the sequels *Good Wives*, *Little Men* and *Jo's Boys*. She wrote about the same family through the generations, following their escapades over the course of Jo's lifetime.

It's always fascinating to track characters over time, to see how they change, and which fundamental characteristics they hold on to their whole lives. You can see this in stories that play out over a longer time period: Richard Linklater's magnificent film *Boyhood*, Evelyn Waugh's novel *Brideshead Revisited*, Khaled Hosseini's beautiful book *The Kite Runner*, and the Stephen Sondheim/George Furth musical *Merrily We Roll Along*.

Today's task is to imagine a pair of siblings, and to write three scenes in which we see them at three different points in their lives. You can include other characters if you want. Consider how their relationship might change. Try to create a journey for them over the course of three scenes, separated by at least a decade. Treat it like a beginning, middle and end. Perhaps they are close as children, they catastrophically fall out as young adults, and they forgive each other when they reach old age.

# 27th August

*"Don't feel guilty if you don't know what you want to do with your life... some of the most interesting forty-year-olds I know still don't."*

Baz Luhrmann, 'Everybody's Free (To Wear Sunscreen)'

Inspired by Baz's wise words, I want you to write a list of all the things you want to do in your life that you haven't done yet. Think big. Which continents do you want to visit? What huge ambitions do you have for future projects? Great things you want to read – and write? And also think small. What do you want to eat more of? Who do you want to hang out with more? Which style of dance do you want to book lessons in? How much time do you want to save by not ironing stuff, and instead using that time to do something fun and creative? Put everything on the list, then divide it into:

1. Things you want to do now.

2. Things you want to do this month.

3. Things you want to do this year.

4. Things you want to do before you're... (pick an age).

Keep on coming back to this list. Don't forget about it... Achieving these things – the big and the small – *will* make your life better.

# 28th August

*"Dialogue is the most fun to write.
It's kind of like a tennis match."*
Sally Rooney

We're going to take Sally Rooney's quote to heart (she knows what she's talking about) and *literally* write a tennis match – or another two-person sport/game/pursuit of your choice.

Write a dialogue scene in which the two characters bounce off each other, scoring points, competing, both in the game and in the conversation. For inspiration, take a look at the zingy dialogue in films like *When Harry Met Sally*, *Bringing Up Baby*, *The Awful Truth*; the plays of Oscar Wilde, Jez Butterworth, Miriam Battye or Richard Bean; and the TV writing of Amy Poehler and Tina Fey.

Give both characters a strong motivation – what do they want? One-upmanship is often the name of the game here. Perhaps they're flirting, perhaps they're making a deal, or trying to do the other over. Either way, pick a fun scenario in which your two protagonists both want to win, and write this as an active scene. Look at how each can 'score points' conversationally and when it might be fun to use that to increase the drama (and potentially the comedy) of your scene.

# 29th August

The locations in your writing are so much more than literal places. A well-written setting can become a character in its own right. Think how much certain places mean to you, and how much one's relationship with a location can tell us about a character and their history.

Today's exercise is to write a scene or passage in which a character returns for the first time to a place that's meant something to them in the past. But rather than picking the obvious place – home, school, university – start the exercise by choosing an unusual location. A phone box, the corner of a football field, an elevator in a hotel, Totteridge & Whetstone Tube station. Then work out which character might be returning there and why.

You may well find that by doing this simple exercise, you suddenly realise you have a whole plot.

# 30th August

*"What terrified me will terrify others; and I need only describe the spectre which had haunted my midnight pillow... Invention, it must be humbly admitted, does not consist in creating out of void, but out of chaos; the materials must, in the first place, be afforded: it can give form to dark, shapeless substances, but cannot bring into being the substance itself."*
Mary Shelley, Introduction to *Frankenstein*

Today's writing prompt is inspired by Mary Shelley's Gothic classic *Frankenstein*. Jump straight in: your task is to write a short story called 'The Creature'. Hint: it doesn't have to be horror. It could be any genre. Horror will be fun. But what sort of short story might 'The Creature' be if it's a romantic comedy? Go wild, take the title to mean whatever you want it to.

# 31st August

*"I don't really decide what the core of the story is before I write. I write to figure out what the story is. And I think the characters end up talking to you and telling you what they want to be doing and what is important to them. So in some ways, your job is to listen as much as it is to write."*
Greta Gerwig

Today, have a go at listening to some characters. Pick two of the following 'voices' and put them together in a scene. Begin writing the dialogue, don't overthink it and don't plan, just see what they say:

- The first woman in space.

- A London Underground driver.

- A grandma who is a part-time spy.

- A war correspondent.

- A calligrapher.

- A dog-walker with twelve dogs in tow.

- A DNA expert.

# September

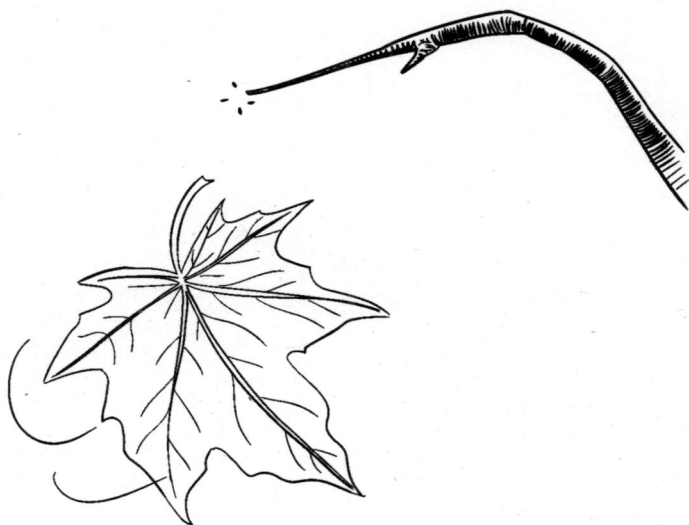

# 1st September

Hooray for autumn, delicious autumn! Today's is a simple task. Write, in any form, about what autumn *feels* like to you. Your feelings, your memories, your associations. And don't get stuck in the trap of thinking you need to be poetic. For some people, autumn is tough, hot and oppressive, the worst time to be working. For others, it's the one chance to take a break. Or perhaps it's the month of 'that memory'. Be personal. What is, how is, who is autumn to you?

SEPTEMBER

# 2nd September

*"He found himself wondering at times, especially in the autumn, about the wild lands, and strange visions of mountains that he had never seen came into his dreams."*
J. R. R. Tolkien, *The Fellowship of the Ring*

**J. R. R. Tolkien** died on this day, so here is a little nod to a man with a wonderful imagination and approach to storytelling.

Tolkien's stories are always beefy and muscular with a really robust plot to dive into. Today we're going to plan a scene with a 'well-made' structure: the classic beginning, middle and ending.

Write down three major plot points of a simple scenario with a pleasant outcome. For example, a girl goes to visit her grandma for tea. The grandma finds out the girl has been misbehaving (let's say, doing drugs), and promises to help her sort her life out by offering her a job as her gardener.

Now, choose one of your story points to flip. You're going to stop your story becoming predictable by sending the plot in the completely contrary direction. Choose the opposite to happen. Or throw in something that breaks the mould.

For example, let's have the young girl discover that her *grandma* is doing drugs! And therefore the girl tries to prevent her grandma getting into trouble by persuading her to come and volunteer at her school with the gardening club. This is much more dramatic and fun because we all expect it'll be the girl who's misbehaving, not the granny.

It's surprising how often these pivots are the moment that make your story really come alive. Be brave in choosing your 'flip' – it will undoubtedly enhance the narrative.

# 3rd September

**Caryl Churchill,** born on this day, is a theatrical goddess, and if you haven't read her work then there's your task for today. Go and do it right now. Read and learn. She is a master, and rewrote all the rules of theatre.

If you don't know where to begin, her play *Love and Information* is a great starting point. It's a series of short scenes, mostly unrelated to each other, which all express something on the theme(s) of the title.

Some of the scenes are only last a few seconds, but look how much life is contained in just a handful of lines, and how little we need to know about the characters to be immediately absorbed in their story. We don't know their names, or anything about them, but it's gripping:

*'Doctor, one thing before I go. Can you tell me how long I've got?*

*There's not an exact answer to that.*

*I'd be grateful for anything you can give me an idea.*

*Well let me say ten per cent of people with this condition are still alive after three years.*

*That's helpful, thank you.'*

That's the whole scene – brilliant, right? And here's another called 'Virtual'… see if you can guess what it's about –

*'I don't care what you say*

*No but listen*

*I've never felt like this*

*That's not the point what you feel*

*It's the only*

*Because she doesn't exist.'*

Your task today is to write two scripts, a maximum of five lines each, that capture a moment in life that is profound and game-changing. Try to leave a degree of mystery and, remember, you don't have to complete the scene, you can leave it on a cliffhanger. Often that will make it the most absorbing. And then go and read the whole of *Love and Information* and fall in love with Caryl Churchill if you haven't already. What a treat you have in store!

# 4th September

*"A stage play is basically a form of uber-schizophrenia. You split yourself into two minds – one being the protagonist and the other being the antagonist. The playwright also splits himself into two other minds: the mind of the writer and the mind of the audience."*
David Mamet

Writing for theatre is a particular art. In theatre, dialogue is king. As a writer it is the only thing you control. A director can choose to interpret your play any way they want, and can – and will often – liberally ignore any stage directions you write, no matter how bold your typeface. Trust me. I've been the put-out writer *and* the determined director in that scenario, and it'll always be the way. But the dialogue… that's different.

Contractually, when a theatre takes on a play they are obliged to stage it word for word as written. Hoorah! The opposite of film, when the script is often torn to shreds, and even after it's been shot, more of it will end up on the cutting-room floor.

So, if you're writing a play: dialogue. That's your job. And it is the most fun!

Today you're going to write a scene for two characters. In order to make it interesting, these two characters know each other already, so we can jump into a pre-existing relationship rather than both of them having to learn everything about each other. Now, our characters need specific aims (motivation) – and to give the scene edge, set those aims at odds with each other.

One person has something the other wants. One person knows something that the other doesn't. One person has a reason not to trust the other. Choose a scenario with naturally high stakes: a wedding, the cockpit of a plane, a graduation day, the final of a contest, a dangerous bridge. Why are your characters there, what do they want, and how is one of them going to win over the other… and is there a spanner you can throw in the works to give it a twist? Enjoy writing it, specifically the dialogue. Write a first pass, where you focus on plotting it out. Now you've worked out what happens, go back and edit, taking out any moment where characters specifically talk about their feelings, and try to get them to say or do something that *demonstrates* this without having to use clunky exposition.

She doesn't need to say 'I'm furious with you' if she's smashing chilli peppers to make a margarita, hammering them into oblivion. That's a much more interesting way to tell that story. Try to give your scene a structure so that it has a beginning, middle and ending. Make sure something fundamentally *changes* by the end of the scene.

Now do another pass, focusing on the dialogue. How do these people speak? What are the characteristics of their voices and what does that reveal about their characters?

# 5th September

*"Every leaf speaks bliss to me,*
*Fluttering from the autumn tree."*
Emily Brontë, 'Fall, leaves, fall'

Today, find a thesaurus and flick through it. Write down twenty words you don't know, what they mean and a bunch of their synonyms. Pick interesting ones. Try to include them in your vocabulary going forward.

# 6th September

*"I am not afraid to write a terrible first draft; in fact, it's very comforting for me to finish a draft no matter how bad it is... A lot of the time what inspires me is just reading something that is totally different from anything I would ever write."*
Emily Henry

Today's task is to create a literary inspiration board – a Pinterest board, if that's your thing. Or you can go 'old school' and make one using paper, photos, cuttings, clippings, objects, and anything you fancy decorating it with. Pin up anything that inspires you, then look at how all the elements add up. What links them? What's the narrative? Write down a list of all the story elements that you can draw from your board...

# 7th September

...and today, write the story, passage or poem that was inspired by yesterday's board! Or, if you'd rather, create a comic-strip story to express this new narrative in a pictorial form. That's it. Go for gold and interpret this any way you want.

SEPTEMBER

# 8th September

*"How vain it is to sit down to write
when you have not stood up to live."*
Henry David Thoreau

Writing in a character's voice convincingly isn't only about capturing the way they speak; it's as much about seeing the world from their unique perspective. So let's practise!

Pick a character – let's call them Juno – then choose a second character who is going to describe Juno. How do they see Juno? Judge them? Feel about them? What details do they notice? What does the way our character describes Juno tell us about a) their relationship and b) the personality of the describer?

Once you've done this, pick a new character to describe Juno – someone else whom Juno may know. Repeat the exercise, then do it one final time with one more describer. Think about how voice and observation can both be used as tools to create characters and relationships.

# 9th September

*"Everyone thinks of changing the world,
but no one thinks of changing himself."*
Leo Tolstoy

Today is the great Russian novelist **Leo Tolstoy's birthday**, so in his honour, today you're going to read the entirety of *War and Peace*. That's a joke. Don't panic.

Actually, you're going to write a short story or passage about an author. Think about who this author might be, where they are writing (if they *are* writing!), when, why, and what is the drama – both in your story and in their writing. You're welcome to write in the first person, if you don't mind it all getting a bit meta.

Enjoy the fact there are two stories to knit together here – the story of the author and the story that the author is writing.

# 10th September

*"The difficultly lies not so much in developing new ideas as in escaping from old ones."*
John Maynard Keynes

Sometimes it's really hard to get out of your usual patterns when you're trying to think of new ideas. So, in order to avoid that, don't think of one yourself. You're going to ask someone else for an idea for a scenario, a brand-new writing prompt, a single sentence of their choice – and your task is to accept whatever they offer you, and go with it!

SEPTEMBER

# 11th September

*"I can never decide whether my dreams are the result of my thoughts or my thoughts the result of my dreams."*
D. H. Lawrence

Apparently **D. H. Lawrence**, whose birthday was today, liked to climb mulberry trees at night... with no clothes on... because it 'helped him write' (really?!) and tickled his imagination. I prefer oak trees, personally. Sturdier branches and more foliage to cover your bits.

So today's task is to climb a tree – just for fun – and see how it makes you feel. Who does it put you in mind of? What character might do this? And if you don't have a tree to climb, choose something equally as daring (though not dangerous, please) – and do the same.

SEPTEMBER

# 12th September

*"Imperfection is beauty, madness is genius, and it's better to be absolutely ridiculous than absolutely boring."*
Marilyn Monroe

Today, write down the ten silliest premises you can for a short story. If you're stuck for inspiration, try picking a random object, an abstract concept and an unexpected character – and challenge yourself to fit them into the same story. For example, a 1950s movie poster, the theme of floating, and a buttoned-up schoolteacher. Or a very narrow mountain path, the notion of 'sparkling', and a six-year-old orphan. How are you going stick those together?!

Plot your basic story. Then expand it, add something even more outlandish, a new factor. A spanner in the works. Perhaps an actual spanner? Or a second character – a talking puffin, perhaps, or a monk who lives in an elevator.

Now have a go at writing it. What's the worst that can happen?!

# 13th September

One of the greatest contributions that Roald Dahl made to literature was the fantastical vocabulary he brought to his work – from 'whizzpoppers' and 'frobscottle' to 'scrumdiddlyumptious', he *loved* using the sound and texture of words to create vivid images in his readers' minds.

Today, on **Roald Dahl's birthday,** stretch your imagination by making up new words for the following things. Think about the shape of a sound in your mouth, and try to reflect the tone of the object in your choices:

- Huge

- Cheese grater

- Wonderful

- Very long road

- Stinking

- Bathrobe

- Granny hat

- Witch

- Fart

- Scared

- Dream

…and then pick some of your own.

# 14th September

*"I write to discover what I know."*
Flannery O'Connor

Take the person you know best in the world: that's you.

Now step outside and write about yourself, but from an external perspective. The narrator is looking in through a window at you. Imagine you know nothing about you – so this is about observing as a stranger from the outside. Scrub all your self-knowledge away!

Imagine watching yourself through a window. Observe yourself really closely. What is the person in the window (i.e. you!) doing? How do they move? Are they talking to someone? Something? A pet? Or themselves? Are they distracted? Relaxed? Busy? Are they singing? Muttering? Dancing? Eating? If so, what are they eating, how are they eating it, and what does that tell you? Do they look like they're going somewhere? If so, what indicates that, and what does it tell you about their hobbies, profession or lifestyle? What do their clothing choices tell you? Are they professional? Artistic? Fearful of the cold? A sun-worshipper? A lover of comfort? A fashionista?

What can we tell from the outside?

SEPTEMBER

# 15th September

*"The best time for planning a book
is while you're doing the dishes."*
Agatha Christie

If **Agatha Christie** lived by this mantra, then boy, she must have had a mighty clean house; she was a truly prolific writer, she wrote at least eighty books, maybe more. And today was her birthday.

She was evidently superhuman. I have no intention of trying to write this much, ever, and if you value having a life, neither should you. But between us, we can definitely write *some* words, perhaps even a book or two.

There's truth in what she says, though. We often have the best ideas when we're not sitting at a desk trying to hash them out. So choose a job. Maybe cleaning. Maybe some other chore. And ask yourself this question: 'Where would I like my story to exist?' Think of places. Places you know, places you'd like to know, near places, far places, real places, fantasy places. And – between washing plates – start to dream about who you might like to meet there. Who is this character? And then – who would *they* encounter there? Someone else who is there for a reason.

Have a think about this simple scenario. A place, a character and a second character who arrives with an objective. Maybe they have information to give to character A. Or a bone to pick. Or maybe it's a reunion. Or a tryst. Or a duel. Who knows? You do!

Don't overthink it. Wash your pots – and as you do, allow yourself to mull on that scenario a bit. When you're done, and the pans are sparkling, sit down and make a few notes. Stick it in your notebook and some time come back to it, and it might spark something. And if it doesn't – hey, you wrote something today; you got your writing muscle working and your kitchen looks smashing. Well done.

# 16th September

On this day in 1985, Kate Bush released her album ***Hounds of Love***. She is, of course, a brilliant musician, but what really caught people's imaginations was her ability to tell a story through song.

So, for today's exercise, set a timer for fifteen minutes.

Pick a short song, or part of a song, you like and know well. Now, keeping the same tune and music, you're going to write entirely original lyrics for this song, under its new title, 'Hounds of Love'.

What might 'Hounds of Love' mean to you? And how different might the spirit of your new song be from the original version? Change the context of a word or a sentence and it really can come to mean something entirely different.

# 17th September

*"When I sit down to write a book, I do not say to myself,
'I am going to produce a work of art.' I write it because there
is some lie that I want to expose,
some fact to which I want to draw attention."*
George Orwell

Today we're going to play around with unusual narrators. We're so used to selecting the most obvious protagonist as the narrative voice, but why not be bold in making a more interesting choice?

For inspiration, grab a copy of Ian McEwan's *Nutshell*, which is written entirely from the perspective of an unborn child. From his mother's womb, he listens to what's going on in the world outside. And it's brilliant.

Take a story you're really familiar with. Fairy stories are easy, good options. And choose a new, truly surprising narrator, not just 'the baddie'. What if Cinderella is retold from the perspective of the glass slipper, for example? Now, rather than attempting the whole story, pick a relevant scene that gives your narrator something interesting to engage with: maybe the scene of trying on the shoes. Cinderella becomes a bit part and can be viewed from the outside. How does the shoe feel about her? Maybe our shoe doesn't like her at all!

SEPTEMBER

# 18th September

*"Composing is like driving down a foggy road toward a house. Slowly you see more details of the house – the colour of the slates and bricks, the shape of the windows. The notes are the bricks and mortar of the house."*
Benjamin Britten

In order to write in another person's voice – to *think* as them – you really need to step into their shoes. Your task today is to create a new character from an outfit you put together. Go to your wardrobe (or your housemate's/children's/partner's wardrobe) or any dressing-up box you have, and pull together a complete outfit to create a different person. If you have the time, go to a charity shop and create a look from what you can find (more fun, plus you get the benefit of donating to a good cause and feeling good!).

Put the outfit on and take some time to think yourself into that character. Shoes particularly help as they make you stand differently. Take a walk around your house. Test how this person sits, stands, what they notice, how they speak. Maybe even take them on a trip out and about, to a shop. What do they buy? How do they interact with people? Remember all these details and scribble them down. They'll be useful tomorrow...

# 19th September

"*However you disguise novels, they are always biographies.*"
William Golding

After yesterday's costuming adventures, today you're going to write a short piece as the character you created.

Now you know how they look, think carefully about how they speak. Are they to-the-point or verbose? On the back foot, shy and stuttering, or brash and confident? Do they speak in full sentences? Are they articulate and clear, or does it take them a while to finish a thought? Do they love to use metaphor, description; do they delight in language? Or do they speak in a straightforward, plain way? Do they have a heritage that means their speech is peppered with words from another culture or country? Do they speak in a dialect? How old are they, and how does that affect their manner of speech?

All these choices can help inform who this person is. It isn't just the content of speech that defines a character, but the way they say it.

For reference and inspiration, check out some great first-person writing in a specific voice. Try *The Girl with the Louding Voice* by Abi Daré – it's mesmeric. Or Roddy Doyle's Irish-English *The Commitments*. Or plays by debbie tucker green or Ntozake Shange.

# 20th September

*"The trick is to go off on your own and finish it.
Separate yourself from others. Toilets are good for that."*
Paul McCartney

Today is a simple writing-prompt day – and your task is to write about:

*The terrible mistake.*

# 21st September

*"Poetry is just the evidence of life.*
*If your life is burning well, poetry is just the ash."*
Leonard Cohen

It's **Leonard Cohen's birthday** – so let's recognise the great lyricist and musician by using his inspiration to kick off today's exercise.

Cohen's song lyrics are like poetry – in fact, they *are* poetry. He described his mind as a messy place, and explained that he needed to simplify his environment in order to find his creative space. He knew what worked for him and he made it happen.

Today, go and listen to one of his songs. Sit and really listen to the words. He is a master storyteller. Your task is to write a poem or song using a line of your choice from his lyrics as your own opening line.

SEPTEMBER

# 22nd September

*"Words and pictures are yin and yang. Married, they produce a progeny more interesting than either parent."*
Dr. Seuss

**National Doodle Day** is in late September. So here's today's task.

Turn to a fresh page in your notebook. Draw a dot. Don't take your pen off the paper. Now start to doodle without lifting your pen, so that you are drawing one long continuous line. Start to shape this line into some form of person. Or creature. Or whatever it might be. You are doodling a spontaneous character. By not taking your pen off the page, you have less control over your image – and spontaneity is the spice in the creative curry… Keep going until you are happy with your creation.

Now take a good look at the character and write down anything you imagine about them. Who is this bearded woman and what does she eat? Where does this slender dancer come from and why do they look so unhappy? What is wrong with this bulbous creature and is that a packet of crisps it's eating?

Now give your character a name, and either write or draw a short piece called *A Day in the Life of* [their name].

# 23rd September

*"When your story is ready for rewrite, cut it to the bone. Get rid of every ounce of excess fat. This is going to hurt; revising a story down to the bare essentials is always a little like murdering children, but it must be done."*
Stephen King

Today, write a descriptive passage about something that happens at sunset. Go to town making it descriptive and detailed – though do remember to make sure something *happens*.

Now follow Stephen King's words of wisdom. Cut away at it. '*Get rid of every ounce of excess fat.*' Reduce it to its very minimal form, being even meaner with your imaginary editorial scissors than you think you ought to be.

Compare the two paragraphs. Which is better? And what's the balance – what is your ideal style, in terms of description versus simplicity?

# 24th September

**F. Scott Fitzgerald**'s writing is brilliant partly because it isn't overwritten. He describes situations vividly but with a smartness and sparseness that means we really pay attention, rather than using florid language which weighs down the narrative.

One way to do this, he advises, is to use verbs, not adjectives, to keep your sentences moving. *'About adjectives: all fine prose is based on the verbs carrying the sentences. They make sentences move.'*

Today, on Fitzgerald's birthday, write a paragraph about a party. A big party, a glitzy one, full of people and excitement. Try to bring it to life, considering all the elements which make this party vibe. The music, costumes, delectable buffet, outlandish characters.

Then edit it for adjectives and try to replace them. You can tell us about a character's attitude through telling us what they're doing, rather than giving us a lot of disposable details about what they're wearing to the party.

# 25th September

*"Get it down. Take chances. It may be bad,
but it's the only way you can do anything really good."*
William Faulkner

We all have off-days, but if you don't persevere, you won't give yourself the chance to be creative at all. As **William Faulkner**, born today, said: 'Get it down.'

So today, write a note to yourself and in it list ten benefits of creativity. Be more specific if you want (if writing is your thing) or, if you'd rather, keep it wide and list the more general benefits of the daily use of your imagination.

Perhaps being creative every day gives you time out for yourself. Or maybe it fulfils a long-standing love: as a child you always wanted to be a novelist but it seemed an impossible dream, but now you're doing the thing you love again! Or maybe it might be simply that it's fun. And fun every day is excellent.

Stick your list somewhere you can see it, and come back to it when you start to feel you're not getting anywhere.

SEPTEMBER

# 26th September

*"Immature poets imitate; mature poets steal."*
T. S. Eliot

Today I am going to follow **T. S. Eliot**'s advice (it's his birthday after all): to be mature and *steal* an exercise from my favourite radio show – because it's wonderful.

*Desert Island Discs*, one of the BBC's longest-running and most popular radio programmes, invites its guests to choose eight songs that they would choose to take with them if they were marooned on a desert island. Some simply pick their favourite songs, but most pick songs that reflect moments, events, phases or people in their life.

Try it for yourself. List your eight songs – and write a line or two about why each has made the playlist. It's a surprisingly emotional exercise, and nearly impossible to choose!

Consider then, how listening to music can alter your mood, and try using it more often within your creative process. Writing a sad scene, for example, ain't gonna be helped by playing Bananarama in the background.

# 27th September

Rachel Carson, a biologist and science writer, wrote **Silent Spring**, published this day in 1962. Taking as its theme the environment and the use of pesticides, it quickly became a *New York Times* bestseller and has been hailed by many as the work that kick-started the environmental movement. Its title comes from a line in John Keats' poem, 'La Belle Dame sans Merci', which powerfully evokes a ruined environment.

Today, keeping Carson's theme in mind, pick a line from Keats' poem to prompt a piece of writing. It can take any form: prose, poetry, drama or non-fiction. Here are a couple of verses (the whole poem is available online if you want to read it all – highly recommended!):

*'I met a lady in the meads*
*Full beautiful, a faery's child;*
*Her hair was long, her foot was light,*
*And her eyes were wild.*

*I set her on my pacing steed,*
*And nothing else saw all day long;*
*For sideways would she lean, and sing*
*A faery's song.*

*I made a garland for her head,*
*And bracelets too, and fragrant zone;*
*She looked at me as she did love,*
*And made sweet moan.*

*She found me roots of relish sweet,*
*And honey wild, and manna dew;*
*And sure in language strange she said,*
*I love thee true.*

*She took me to her elfin grot,*
  *And there she gazed and sighed deep,*
*And there I shut her wild sad eyes –*
  *So kissed to sleep.*

*…And this is why I sojourn here*
  *Alone and palely loitering,*
*Though the sedge is withered from the lake,*
  *And no birds sing.'*

# 28th September

"You can't base your life on other people's expectations."
Stevie Wonder

And Stevie said that *before* the advent of social media! Let's embrace social media – not something I'd usually encourage – and use it as inspiration for today's writing. Choose between:

- Taking a post on a social media platform of your choice as a writing prompt.

or

- Finding an interesting Instagram profile and using that person as your protagonist.

If you don't use or have no access to social media (you are wise, my friend), instead select a writer from the letters pages of a magazine or newspaper, and make them your character. People who write to publications can be great fodder for characters as they undoubtedly have strong opinions!

# 29th September

*"Deep down, I know I have this intuition or instinct that a lot of creative people have: that their demons are also what make them create."*
David Byrne

Today we're going to draw inspiration from the outside world. I hope you have access to the internet – if you do, your task is to use a TED Talk as a prompt. TED is an organisation that curates speakers on hundreds of different topics, all experts in their fields, and gives them a short platform (usually ten minutes) to share their work and experience.

Listening to TED Talks is one of the simplest ways to expand your knowledge of the world in the *widest* sense, by listening to impassioned experts on any subject you could imagine.

So today, watch three TED Talks that you feel are outside your usual knowledge pool and have a listen. Then, choose one, and use it as a jumping-off point for a piece of writing. Perhaps you want to dramatise an anecdote. Or imagine a character affected by the issue of the talk. For inspiration, why not start with the exceptional Jill Bolte Taylor's 'My Stroke of Insight' or Dave Eggers' 'My Wish: Once Upon a School'.

# 30th September

*"To me, the greatest pleasure of writing is not what it's about, but the inner music that words make."*
Truman Capote

**Truman Capote**, born today, pioneered and popularised a new form of novel when he wrote *In Cold Blood*. It's a non-fiction novel – so a novelisation of an actual event – with the events carefully researched in order to be as close as possible to the factual truth. The book is a retelling of the murders of four members of the Clutter family in 1959, and, in order to write accurately, Capote went to Kansas to immerse himself in the story and to interview the community and investigators. It took him six years to gather the requisite research and finish the book.

You don't have six years for this task – you have one day, but you're going to use the same principles. Think of a dramatic real-life event – or check the news – and spend an hour reading everything that you can about it. Write down every detail. Make sure, as part of your research, you read interviews – you need to be able to tune into the voices of the participants.

Now write your short story in narrative prose, using your research. Remember that truth is often stranger (and more engaging) than fiction, so the more factual detail you include, the richer your writing will be.

# October

# 1st October

It's **International Coffee Day!**

Coffee. Delicious. And often the reason I do (or don't) get enough work done.

Today, rather than letting making a coffee become a distraction, let's make it the focus of your task.

Make a cup of coffee. Sit and enjoy it (or hate it, if you don't like coffee). You are going to write the most *in detail* account of the experience of drinking the coffee as you can. Write as you drink. Every detail. Think specifically about the experience of the initial smell, the taste on the different parts of your tongue, the sensation of the swallow, the effect it has on you. Detail, detail, detail. If you don't like coffee this will be a particularly interesting piece (sorry).

OCTOBER

# 2nd October

Today you're going to pick an everyday object and write a 'day in its life'.

Personify it. Where does it live and how is it used? How does it feel about being used/ignored/overused? Who is using it? And how do they treat it? Does it get treated worse by some people (swiftly grabbed, chewed, tossed aside) than by others (who lovingly appreciate it)? How does the pencil/loofah/fridge feel about that? What kind of mood is your object in, and does that change? And what does it feel like to be it? What's its future? Is it having an existential crisis or is it happy with its lot?

Choose an object that naturally has engaging interactions. A sink tap in a rundown station toilet sees more life, for example, than an object stuck in a drawer... though said object will likely have dramatic opinions about their unfortunate situation.

# 3rd October

*"Architecture is like writing.
You have to edit it over and over so it looks effortless."*
Zaha Hadid

**World Architecture Day** is always the first Monday in October, so, if it's not today, it'll be this week – let's celebrate it anyway!

Yesterday we chose an inanimate object as a character and wrote a day in its life. Today's exercise, an extension, is going *big* in comparison. No more pencil sharpeners or kettles, today you're going to pick a building.

Choose one with an interesting history – because you're going to write from its perspective *across time*. If it is an ancient Pyramid, what has it seen? A crumbling Elizabethan cottage? A Hollywood mansion in Beverly Hills? What surrounds it? How has that changed over the years? Who has lived in it, or visited it, and how does it feel about them? You could perhaps pick three moments in its history to reflect on. Or do as you please. As every character has a backstory, so does every building.

If you like, you can draw the building in its three different moments as a jumping-off exercise.

# 4th October

Today you're going to try to make someone cry.

No, not in real life. I don't want to be responsible for that! Instead, you're going to write a scene that touches a real place of sadness. Imagine that your character is looking at a photograph. Write the scene that stems from this – with a focus on the melancholy. Try to find the greatest heart and poignancy in the story. The photograph should make your protagonist profoundly sad – or provoke this in the reader. Who is the person looking at the photograph and what do they see that affects them so profoundly?

# 5th October

Limericks. Remember them? Many of us studied them at school. It's a form of storytelling verse with the strict rhyme scheme AABBA, and it's most often either witty or rude, hopefully both. It often begins 'There was a young…' But it doesn't have to.

> There was a young lady from Fratton,
> Who liked to be seen with her hat on,
> But she had to give in,
> When once, on the gin,
> She fell flat and her hat was too sat on.

Write a limerick about a person. Perhaps someone from the town where you live or you grew up. Or a funny one about a misogynistic ticket inspector who gets his comeuppance, or a reviled schoolteacher. Feel free to make it rude. Time to get your own back for boring school lessons.

OCTOBER

# 6th October

*"'If you knew Time as well as I do,' said the Hatter,
'you wouldn't talk about wasting it.'"*
Lewis Carroll, *Alice's Adventures in Wonderland*

Having an eye on time – specifically the timeline of your plot – is an essential part of good storytelling. Playing your story over the course of a single night, for example, can add tension and excitement. Or plotting a narrative that returns to characters over a span of years allows you to dive deeper into their trajectories as they grow older and gain life experience… Whether they use this experience or not is up to you!

Today, pick a character that you have already been writing about, and create a timeline of the significant moments in their life. I like to draw it as a graph across several sheets of paper. In film, we often use Post-it notes and stick them on the wall, so that you can move them around and add other moments in between, as you think of them.

If you're using Post-its you can make use of their various colours. Pink for things that happen to the character. Yellow for things that happen to other characters in their life, which still influence your protagonist. Blue for world events that impact your story.

When you're done, take a view on which part of your timeline you're most interested in. Maybe that's the story you really want to tell. Where do you jump in and out for maximum impact? Might you use other key moments in your story too: flashbacks to a younger self, for example? Or do you want an epilogue showing your character at the end of their timeline, looking back? Stay open to dropping into different moments if it helps your story. Sometimes it's a wonderful way to illuminate a character.

OCTOBER

# 7th October

*"We are all apprentices in a craft
where no one ever becomes a master."*
Ernest Hemingway, *The Wild Years*

There is one company who seem to have nailed the backbone of a well-made dramatic tale – and this is Pixar, the great animation studio. Watch any of their films and the storytelling is masterful: great tales filled with heart, drama, winning protagonists, lots at stake, an exciting conclusion… they understand how to hook an audience.

Aim this week to watch one Pixar film: *Toy Story, Finding Nemo, Up* or *Inside Out*, for example. Every film of theirs follows the same basic (genius) formula. A protagonist is thrown into a quandary when something big happens to them. This propels them to take action, and to eventually change something, solve a problem, be the hero. Usually this involves a wider dramatic situation *and* dealing with their own personal flaws at the same time. Here's the formula:

1. Once upon a time there was ___. (The set-up: who and what?)

2. Every day, ___. (The character's world before the change.)

3. One day ___. (The big change!)

4. Because of that, ___. (Their journey.)

5. Because of that, ___. (What they face and how they face it.)

6. Until finally ___. (How they achieve their goal – or don't – and what they learn.)

Your task today is to take three films you know well, and test out whether they fit this Pixar formula. Try to fill in each story point for each narrative. You'll be surprised how well it is likely to work. Remember that the obstacles can be psychological rather than physical strife; often what a hero faces is an internal fear or prejudice, rather than an earthquake.

# 8th October

*"I was a product of Andy Warhol's Factory.
All I did was sit there and observe these incredibly talented
and creative people who were continually making art,
and it was impossible not to be affected by that."*
Lou Reed

Yesterday we looked at storytelling formula through *observing* other people's work and analysing their film stories. Today, you're going to do your own! Use yesterday's six-point Pixar formula to tell your own original story. Begin by setting out your story into the six beats, then either write it, or draw it as a storyboard sequence. Go!

# 9th October

*"A letter always seemed to me like immortality*
*because it is the mind alone without corporeal friend."*
Emily Dickinson

Choose a famous person, someone on the world stage, past or present. Today, on **World Post Day**, you're going to write a letter from them… to someone we wouldn't expect.

We are so used to hearing of well-known people mixing within their elite circles, but not today! Instead, choose someone outside this predictable bubble as the surprising receiver. Maybe Shirley Bassey is writing to a music teacher who helped her learn how to sing. Maybe Jackie Kennedy is writing to her housekeeper in Martha's Vineyard. Maybe Helen Mirren is writing to her milkman, who has become her greatest confidant.

Try to bring in a sense of the lives of both letter-writer and recipient. Where are the similarities, despite their vastly different trajectories? It is essential if you're writing real people, especially royalty or major world figures, to understand their vulnerabilities, to make it clear that they are essentially exactly like the rest of us. That's what will allow us to empathise – and that's what makes good writing.

# 10th October

"I think we communicate only too well, in our silence, in what is unsaid, and that what takes place is a continual evasion, desperate rear-guard attempts to keep ourselves to ourselves. Communication is too alarming. To enter into someone else's life is too frightening. To disclose to others the poverty within us is too fearsome a possibility."

Harold Pinter

Playwright **Harold Pinter** was the master of the pause. It could be used for tension, for suspense, for comedy, he was able to use pauses and silences to tell us *everything* about what a character was thinking. It's often called a 'pregnant pause' because it's full. Full of meaning; tension, anticipation or excitement.

Today, on his birthday, let's do an exercise inspired by Pinter. There are two people in a room. One standing by the door, the other sitting down. There is nothing in the room but the two people and the chair. Who are they? What are they doing there? Your scene is going to be twelve lines long. After every three lines there is going to be a pause. The characters do not have to take it in turns to speak. You can also use pauses or silence additionally, if a person, for example, doesn't complete their sentence. See what happens… and enjoy the drama that comes from what's *not* being said!

Take a leaf out of Pinter's book – keep your dialogue succinct; less is more in what they say, too. It's much more interesting for a first line to be 'Where did you go?' than 'Come on, Eleanor, I really expected you to be home earlier after tennis, I knew I couldn't trust you, where did you go?' In 'Where did you go?' alone there is a world of possibility. In the second sentence, almost none.

# 11th October

*"I am no bird; and no net ensnares me:*
*I am a free human being with an independent will."*
Charlotte Brontë, *Jane Eyre*

It's **International Day of the Girl,** a brilliant initiative by the United Nations. Because, let's face it, girls are brilliant!

Often having to face prejudice, complicated expectations, unwanted attention and impossible standards, girls have finally found their way into the spotlight in the last few years as people worthy of support and celebration. So let's do that today.

So, write a passage about a twelve-year-old girl. Any girl, from anywhere in the world, from any time in history, in any circumstance that you choose. She could be an illiterate, yet story-loving medieval farmhand. Or the wealthy daughter of an Indian maharajah. Any choice is an interesting choice.

The only rules are to write in her voice. Be specific. Go.

OCTOBER

# 12th October

*"So where do the ideas actually come from? Mostly from getting annoyed about things. Not big issues so much... as the little irritations that drive you wild out of all proportion."*
Douglas Adams

Today in 1979, **The Hitchhiker's Guide to the Galaxy** was published. It's a pretty good title, right?

Today's task is to write the titles of eight books you might like to write one day. Who knows, maybe it's time to start writing one?

# 13th October

*"The idea is to write it so that people hear it and it slides through the brain and goes straight to the heart."*
Maya Angelou

The heart is a universal symbol; as much a part of folklore, myth and iconography as it is also the beating organ keeping us alive.

Today write down five different sentences that include the word 'heart', each in a different context. One might be a biological fact: 'His heart began to race as the hairy tarantula inched its way towards him across the pillow.' Others might be more abstract or symbolic: 'The way the boy looked at him made his heart dance.'

Then, when you're done, write a passage titled 'The Heart' in which you use at least two of these ideas. Intertwining an image both as a literal object and a metaphorical motif can lift your writing away from the everyday towards something more profound.

OCTOBER

# 14th October

Turn on your TV. Write down the first line that you hear and write a story based on it.

# 15th October

*"Haiku is not a shriek, a howl, a sigh, or a yawn;*
*rather, it is the deep breath of life."*
Santōka Taneda

A haiku is a form of short Japanese poem that, traditionally, celebrates nature and aims to say something profound in a minimalist way. Its structure is simple: three lines, seventeen syllables in total. The first line is five syllables; the second, seven; and the final line, five.

The aim is to make the reader appreciate the beauty of the world around us, or better understand the human experience. Santōka explained:

*'Real haiku is the soul of poetry. Anything that is not actually present in one's heart is not haiku. The moon glows, flowers bloom, insects cry, water flows. There is no place we cannot find flowers or think of the moon. This is the essence of haiku. Go beyond the restrictions of your era, forget about purpose or meaning, separate yourself from historical limitations – there you will find the essence of true art, religion and science.'*

Here are a few examples, one that celebrates nature by Matsunaga Teitoku, a Japanese poet (who lived from 1571 to 1654):

*'Many solemn nights*
*Blond moon, we stand and marvel…*
*Sleeping our noons away.'*

And another, by Lauren Beukes (born in 1976):

*'She would disappear*
*folded like origami*
*into her own dreams'*

Beautiful. Try it for yourself. Write three. One about nature, one about your personal experience, and one wildcard – where you can write about anything you want.

# 16th October

*"'Twas brillig, and the slithy toves*
*Did gyre and gimble in the wabe:*
*All mimsy were the borogoves,*
*And the mome raths outgrabe."*
Lewis Caroll, 'Jabberwocky'

Oh Lewis Caroll. The inventor of brilliant words. What a joyful time he must have had writing 'Jabberwocky'. Either joyful or intoxicated. Or both.

Your task today is to write a short poem based on a familiar story. Fairy stories are an easy pick; maybe a fable. Or perhaps a legend, like St George and the Dragon. This will take you out of the real world into somewhere more extraordinary, meaning you can be extra playful with vocabulary invention.

Firstly, write out the bare bones of the story so that you have a clear sense of the plot points – beginning, middle and end. A sentence for each is sufficient. That's your three verses. Next, have a go at writing the poem, using normal vocabulary. It doesn't have to rhyme, of course.

And then – and here's the fun bit – go back and pick out any word you like and replace it with a new, made-up word – the sound of which should evoke the feeling of the word. 'Mimsy' in Carroll's poem, for example, sounds light and delicate, whereas a 'mome rath' sounds frankly terrifying. Start off by changing just a few words, then really go for it. You may well find you've written an entirely new – and far more interesting – tale!

OCTOBER

# 17th October

*"For me poetry is not the exclusive domain of academia.
Stuff to be studied and dissected in college classrooms like
a lab rat to find out what makes it tick. It is a form of human
expression. The transference of human emotion from one
person to another whether it is written or performed."*
Valentine Okolo, *I Will Be Silent*

It's **Black Poetry Day** today. From the genius of Maya Angelou to the triumph of young Amanda Gorman at Joe Biden's presidential inauguration, there is a wealth of poetry by people of colour that deserves great attention.

Today's task is to go and find poems by two different Black poets. Sit, read, enjoy and learn.

OCTOBER

# 18th October

*"It is better to fail in originality than to succeed in imitation."*
Herman Melville

Success in writing is so often about perseverance. Even when you're devoid of inspiration or you think your work sucks, somehow you have to carry on. It's a muscle. If you don't use it, it'll get saggy and limp, and no one wants that. So get motivated.

Today, write down three goals that you have in your writing. Perhaps it's simply to write something every day. Perhaps it's to read a book a month, or join a writing group. Perhaps it's just to complete your daily tasks in this book! Whatever they are, write them down, pin them up somewhere you'll see them every day (mine are my laptop screensaver), and DO THEM!

OCTOBER

# 19th October

*"We don't need a list of rights and wrongs, tables of dos and don'ts: we need books, time and silence. 'Thou shalt not' is soon forgotten, but 'Once upon a time' lasts forever."*
Philip Pullman

In an ode to the simplicity of the Western world's most famous story phrase, let's do what **Philip Pullman,** born today, advises…

Without a list of dos or don'ts, without restriction of any kind, today's task is simply to write a story beginning 'Once upon a time…' Don't plan it. Write freely and without editing yourself, free-writing, until you get to 'The End'.

# 20th October

Originality in writing is so often about presenting something familiar in a way that makes us see it anew. Describing a character we *think* we recognise – and then revealing that they're not what we expect at all.

Today your task is to write a description of the most boring character you can possibly imagine. Consider what is it about this incredibly uninspiring person that makes them the last person you'd make the star of your story. And then… write a story, making them your lead.

'Boring' really can be a fascinating character trait!

OCTOBER

# 21st October

Today you're going to write a stream-of-consciousness piece about your very earliest memory. Feel free to spend a bit of time working out what it is! Find a place where you don't usually write. A place with a different view from whatever you're usually staring at. It could be outside, under a tree, or in a café. Set a timer for ten minutes and just start writing.

Begin by writing down absolutely everything you remember about that memory. Don't edit. Just write every detail – and hopefully each may trigger a little more of a memory to rise up. Think of it as meditative writing, where you are literally recording every thought as it arrives.

Now re-read it and see what interests you. Throw out anything that doesn't, and feel free to elaborate on whatever does. You can now add fictional accoutrements to dramatise your story. So your memory becomes the primary source, and you can now enjoy the creative freedom to do with it what you will.

# 22nd October

Take two characters you are familiar with, either from your own work or from novels, plays or films you know. Pull them from two different sources. Maybe one is a Jane Austen heroine and another is a villain in a Quentin Tarantino movie. Now stick them in a room together and see what happens. Write that scene.

# 23rd October

*"People who do a job that claims to be creative have to be alone to recharge their batteries. You can't live twenty-four hours a day in the spotlight and remain creative. For people like me, solitude is a victory."*
Karl Lagerfeld

Karl is right... up to a point. But I'd argue that often creativity comes from making sure you *are* in the bustling busy-ness, the hubbub, the bubble, taking in what's careering around you, watching, staying hungry for company and inspiration. You always hear things that surprise you. You can't just pull everything out of your head. You need to put fuel in to get the creative engine firing.

So, today's task is to go somewhere really busy, and to watch someone, or two people, or three people. They are going to be your characters. Listen to what they're saying. Watch them carefully, like specimens in a Petri dish. Use this as inspiration for a piece of writing. You are taking in the outside world, and making it your own.

# 24th October

*"Anxiety is the handmaiden of creativity."*
T. S. Eliot

Have you ever had anxiety in anticipation of a major celebration? (A big birthday. A wedding. A party.) And you want to make a great impression?

Your task today is to write an invitation to quash these fears. Not a run-of-the-mill, boring invitation… this is the party everyone wants to go to because you invite guests in a way that will delight them. Do you write in the style of a great Victorian entertainer? Is it cryptic? Is it novelesque? Perhaps the theme of the party can give you a clue.

Enjoy it – and if it inspires you, why not throw the party?! I'll come.

# 25th October

*"Protect the time and space in which you write.*
*Keep everybody away from it,*
*even the people who are most important to you."*
Zadie Smith

It's **Zadie Smith's birthday** today. Dive into her writing tips – they are plentiful and brilliant… and simple, and readily available online.

Like this simple but excellent advice: Disconnect from the internet.

Your task is to cordon off your writing time – today *and* in the future – by writing with your Wi-Fi turned off and your phone put away. Whenever I am working I set an alarm for fifty-two minutes of internet-free time, during which I work solidly without stopping. If I think of something I need to look up or something I need to remember, I write it down on a paper list then carry on with my work. It's the only way I find not to get distracted.

Fifty-two minutes is apparently the optimum concentration period for us humans. Whether that's right or not, I like the randomness of it, and it's worked for me for years.

So put your phone on airplane mode, turn off your computer Wi-Fi, and write for fifty-two minutes. Anything you like. But do it. And if you get stuck, wait it out till you unstick yourself. You will.

# 26th October

Write a detailed description of your favourite item of clothing and why it means so much to you. What's its backstory? What does it look like, feel like, smell like? Why do you love it? See if you can get a full page of writing out of your garment.

OCTOBER

# 27th October

*"And by the way, everything in life is writable about if you have the outgoing guts to do it, and the imagination to improvise. The worst enemy to creativity is self-doubt."*
Sylvia Plath

**Sylvia Plath,** born on this day, wrote exceptional verse. In 'You're', she writes an ode to the unborn child she is carrying. In every line she describes the nature of that child, the way it sits in the womb, in the dark, baking like a loaf, readying to come out – comfortable in the darkness – '*Snug as a bud and at home / Like a sprat in a pickle jug*'. Elsewhere she describes the oddity of its body, still finding beauty in the detail: '*Feet to the stars, and moon-skulled, / Gilled like a fish*'.

The poem's brilliance is in the way she balances beautifully original similes – which find lyricism in the everyday – with something utterly profound. Her love for and anticipation of the unborn child, a maternal bond that is clear in every line.

Today, look the poem up and use it as your inspiration to write about someone you love in your own 'You're' poem. Imagine that every line begins 'You're…' You can read Plath's poem like this, which helps unpack its meaning.

Your challenge is to use metaphors from the everyday world, not universal, 'poetic' imagery about stars and planets, for example. Try to pick metaphors and similes that somehow relate to the person to further explore a theme. Enjoy!

OCTOBER

# 28th October

Today is a simple writing-prompt day – and your task is to write about:

*The experience of falling.*

Start, if you want, by sketching some pictures inspired by the phrase to get your imagination in gear.

OCTOBER

# 29th October

*"Think eight hours, work two hours."*
Mirko Ilić

Ilić has a point. Most good writing comes after a good deal of mulling. Today, set an alarm for eight minutes. After you've started the timer, all you're going to do is think of a story. DO NOT WRITE A WORD. For eight minutes you are just going to sit and imagine. We're not used to doing this, we find it uncomfortable; inevitably you'll start thinking about whether you bought enough gin for tonight or if there's any cheese left, or what was the name of the kid at school who had that weird haircut. That's okay. Minds wander. But get back to it. Keep telling yourself to come back to the story.

After eight minutes, start writing. Write for as long or as little time as you are inspired. Was the thinking time helpful? If it was, lodge it in your writer's toolbox and use it whenever you get stuck (I can heartily recommend heading outside to walk and think).

OCTOBER

# 30th October

*"I think people have to sharpen their eyes and look.
I always feel like a big sponge: I feel like I learn lots of things
by osmosis, and I feel that I'm always absorbing.
I mean, when people say, 'What is your inspiration?' I could
throw up. I mean, I'm inspired by the fact I get up in the
morning. And I'm still here."*
Iris Apfel

Today, you need to find a painting that you find inspiring. If you can get to a gallery, do that. If not, a book or the internet is a good next bet. It must have figures in it. Choose one or two of the people in the painting, and using the emotional tone of the work, write a short story with these characters at the heart of it.

Perhaps the action in the painting dictates the action in the story; you could take the scenario and run with it. Perhaps you might have other ideas. Look closely at the characters, their posture and expressions, their world, and use this as food to fuel your narrative.

# 31st October

*"Terrify yourself at least a little with every new project."*
Kamila Shamsie

Happy **Halloween**! Today you have a choice of tasks – a trick or treat, if you will, depending on what you fancy on this oh-so-auspicious of days.

Did you pick treat? Write a passage about a time in your life you were *genuinely* scared. To create drama, jump into the story as late as you can, and jump out earlier than your instinct tells you… Resist the urge to complete the story, and instead end on a cliffhanger.

Or did you pick trick? Do the same – but you can't use any words beginning with 'T'. Haha! I dare you.

# November

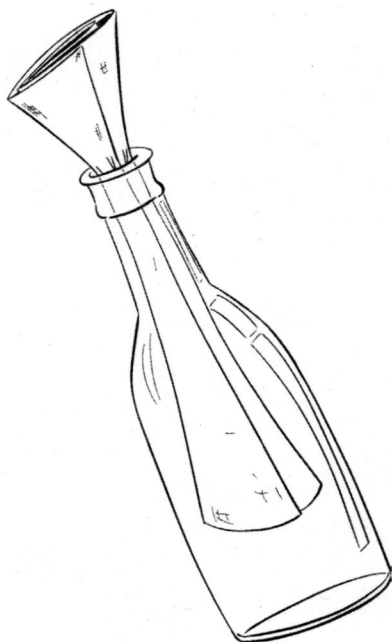

# 1st November

Today you're going to channel the spirit of American poet Allen Ginsberg. Go and read **'Howl'**, published on this day in 1956, a long poem written in a single sentence. It begins with one thought at the start, then expands onwards, in a gathering, growing denunciation of capitalism. Here's just the beginning:

> *'I saw the best minds of my generation destroyed by madness,
>     starving hysterical naked,*
> *dragging themselves through the negro streets at dawn looking for
>     an angry fix,*
> *angelheaded hipsters burning for the ancient heavenly connection to
>     the starry dynamo in the machinery of night,*
> *who poverty and tatters and hollow-eyed and high sat up smoking
>     in the supernatural darkness of cold-water flats floating across
>     the tops of cities contemplating jazz,*
> *who bared their brains to Heaven under the El and saw
>     Mohammedan angels staggering on tenement roofs illuminated'*

…and it continues like this… for quite a while (255 lines to be precise, which is quite something).

So today, you're going to write a thought poem like this. Choose a subject you feel passionately about. It could be something difficult, as 'Howl' is, or something joyous, like a love of cooking Mexican food, or walking in Central Park.

Begin in the first paragraph by setting out your stall, introducing your theme, then continue, as Ginsberg does, to expand and expand on detail. It's an unusual form, but it's a great experiment.

# 2nd November

*"Almost everything will work again*
*if you unplug it for a few minutes... including you."*
Anne Lamott

This week it is **National Stress Awareness Day** – it's the first Wednesday in November, so perhaps it's today. If it's not, don't stress!

So do yourself a favour – and disconnect. Try to survive a whole day away from social media and the internet. Turn off your apps, put your phone in another room, duck out of that Zoom meeting and use the time instead to read a book.

If you can't cope without the distractions, try a shorter period. Spend at least an hour reading a book today. It will feed your mind, boost your soul and lower your stress levels. You're welcome.

NOVEMBER

# 3rd November

*"Clichés can be quite fun. That's how they got to be clichés."*
Alan Bennett, *The History Boys*

A cliché is a tired old phrase that is overused, and therefore has become dull. Poor clichés! And the reason it became overused, of course, because people liked them. What a boon it is to be popular.

So today, as it's **Cliché Day** (I kid you not), we are going to be kind to our familiar friends and embrace them. Your task is to write a passage entirely in clichés. Hey, don't complain. I know 'the grass is always greener', but you've gotta 'think outside the box', and if you 'play your cards right' and write fast you'll be done in a 'shake of a lamb's tail', in 'the blink of an eye', 'quick as a flash', 'faster than a speeding bullet'…

Have a try. It's actually quite hard, and not 'as easy as pie'.

# 4th November

*"You see things; and you say, 'Why?'*
*But I dream things that never were; and I say, 'Why not?'"*
George Bernard Shaw, *Back to Methuselah*

Beginning with 'I remember...', write about a vivid dream you've had. If you struggle to remember your dreams, for the next few nights, leave a notebook by your bed, and write down what you were dreaming every morning as soon as you wake up. (Or in the middle of the night if a vivid dream wakes you up.) You'll find that you quickly begin to remember your dreams better if you get into the habit of writing them down. Otherwise they flit away as quickly as they arrived and they'll be gone forever.

# 5th November

*"Creativity comes from trust. Trust your instincts.
And never hope for it more than you work for it."*
Rita Mae Brown

There are so many great words. Chewy, muscular words; soft and mellifluous words; brisk and sharp words. Today's exercise is to write out the alphabet, A to Z, and think of a fantastic adjective (a 'describing' word) beginning with each letter. Double points if you find one for every letter of the alphabet.

Then look over your list and replace any choices you find uninspiring with something more thrilling. Finally, get your thesaurus out and find a new adjective for every letter – a word you would never usually use. 'Effulgent' for example, or 'rebarbative'.

# 6th November

Or, in other words: 'Strike while the iron is hot!'

What's happening right now in your world? Open the paper. Turn on the news. Pick a story and write about it. Step outside the event and the people involved, and choose an external narrative voice – an onlooker.

Now write the drama as a piece of fiction. Chew on the delicious detail and use the contemporaneous nature of the event to give your piece vim and currency, and perhaps most importantly, a feeling that you are present, imbuing your work with a true sense of immediacy.

# 7th November

"You could write a song about some kind of emotional problem you are having, but it would not be a good song, in my eyes, until it went through a period of sensitivity to a moment of clarity. Without that moment of clarity to contribute to the song, it's just complaining."
Joni Mitchell

Ah, **Joni Mitchell**. What a wonderful, poetic goddess of a woman.

Today, on her birthday, your task is to choose one of her songs, then sit, listen and write. Play the song twice before you write anything. Pay attention to both the lyrics and the melody. Now start writing, but as you do, keep playing the song on repeat, so that it becomes the soundtrack to your writing today. Maybe what you write is inspired by the lyrics, maybe it's the tone and tempo and timbre of the music that sets the emotional tone. Or maybe you're inspired to write about a songwriter as a character. Trust your gut. Write with the music for at least ten minutes, then, if you feel inspired, carry on.

# 8th November

*"As a writer, I'm more interested in what people tell themselves happened rather than what actually happened."*
Kazuo Ishiguro

Today is **Kazuo Ishiguro's birthday**. Inspired by his quote, pick a major event, something that really happened. You could pick a world event, like the fall of the Berlin Wall. Or the discovery of DNA. Or the moment the Event Horizon Telescope took its first image of a black hole. Or the day the first female astronaut went to space (Valentina Tereshkova in 1963). Or, on a smaller scale, perhaps a local triumph or tragedy – something that happened in your community, or in the town where you grew up.

Now think of someone who witnessed this event, or was involved in some way. You're going to write about the event from their perspective (as if they are being interviewed) – but crucially, you must bend the narrative voice to reveal what this person is *telling themselves* happened, rather than what really happened. As Ishiguro says, it's this sense of personal perspective and viewpoint – which is always, in its very nature, biased – that makes for an interesting voice.

# 9th November

Not every day can be a good writing day. So today, go out and observe some stories. Sit in a café, and watch and listen. Go to a busy bus station and take in the stories that are playing out in front of you. If you were a film-maker, what would you try to capture? Where would you point your camera? Who interests you, which scenarios? Seek the drama. And store it in your brain – or write it in your notebook – for another time. You don't have to write anything down; absorbing the characters into your imagination bank can be enough.

NOVEMBER

# 10th November

*"I think every work of art is an act of faith, or we wouldn't bother to do it. It is a message in a bottle, a shout in the dark. It's saying, 'I'm here and I believe that you are somewhere and that you will answer if necessary across time, not necessarily in my lifetime.'"*
Jeanette Winterson

Today, write a message in a bottle. A letter from someone on an island – perhaps to someone specific, perhaps to anyone who finds it. Ask yourself why your writer wants to communicate with a distant shore. Is it an act of desperation, or an invitation to potential island-mates to come and share this idyll? Be as creative and inventive with it as you can. Hey, you can even soak it in tea and write in spidery writing for that 'olde treasure mappe' effect, if that's what floats your boat – no pun intended.

And if you feel *really* inspired, you could always toss it into the waves of the nearest river or sea and see what happens. I am not condoning littering, of course. Think of it as interactive theatre – but with an audience who aren't expecting it.

# 11th November

Writing *is* rewriting, right? That's what they say. And it's true. Good work is carefully crafted, edited, honed, revised, rewritten, critiqued (by you) and revisited multiple times as you strive to get it right. First drafts ought to be ropey – that's why they are first drafts. Always give yourself a free pass to write without judgement when you first put pen to paper.

So today, pull out a piece of writing from earlier in the year and rewrite it. Edit, edit, edit. Improve it, make it better. And enjoy the benefit of the distance you've had from it in giving you perspective.

NOVEMBER

# 12th November

Take a novel off your shelf. Open it at random. Skim your finger across the page and pick a line. This sentence is the first sentence of today's piece of writing. Where will it take you?

# 13th November

Today is **World Kindness Day** (and **Robert Louis Stevenson's birthday,** by the way), so today you're going to do something nice – for yourself! However confidently you present yourself to the outside world, we always have a long list of things we don't like about ourselves, what we'd like to change, reasons why we're not good enough.

So today, write a letter to yourself, as if from a friend's perspective, telling you that you are actually *great.* List all the things you like about yourself. Your qualities. What you – as this 'friend' – admires about you. Then write about your imperfections, anything that make you feel bad about yourself, that you wish you could change – whether it's wobbly thighs or ugly toes or not being as clever/ beautiful/sporty/high-achieving/pregnant/young/famous as you might like to be. Now have the 'friend' explain why these things are actually *just fine.* They're what makes you individual. And who needs to be so high-achieving/gorgeous/young anyway? It must be a real pain in the ass having everyone stare at you all the time. Be kind to yourself. And realise that you are, in fact, excellent.

# 14th November

*"Children are made readers on the laps of their parents."*
Emilie Buchwald

Today, write about something that happened to one of your parents, in their voice. If you're lucky enough to still have them around, ask them – use them as research – find out a story from their past that is new to you and write it in character, in the first person, as them. If you're not able to ask them, try to remember an anecdote they told you. Writing in the voice of someone you know well can be surprisingly difficult! Have a go. And then hang out with them if you have that chance. No one is around forever, and that time is precious.

# 15th November

*"A writer is a world trapped in a person."*
Victor Hugo

It's **'I Love to Write' Day**! So today – choose your own writing task
that you know you'll really enjoy. Which is the task you've enjoyed
the most so far? Try it again – throwing a different idea into the mix.
Be inspired by your own work – and your independence! Go!

Don't all choose 29th January at once!

# 16th November

*"Ideas are cheap, it's the execution that is all important."*
George R. R. Martin

Let's talk about your voice as a writer. It's your hallmark, your unique instrument. And it is particular to you. Sometimes hard to define, it's partly tone, partly outlook, partly style – but a writer's tone always matches, in some way, with their personality. Are you dark and brooding? Are you a serious intellectual? Are you a bright optimist?

Your task today is to describe yourself in a series of adjectives. What are you like? And as you write the list, start thinking about how this might define you as a writer.

Next, write a list to describe your voice. Play around with it – try to think of a wide variety of words, particularly words that would be used to describe the tone of a story, e.g. playful, tense, elegant, compelling, verbose, dreamlike, brusque, witty. If you need inspiration, hop onto Netflix (or another streaming platform), as they always use a series of words to describe the tone of each show. *Stranger Things*, for example, is 'Nostalgic', '80s', 'Sci-fi'.

Now pick your four favourite words from your 'voice' list and use them as a prompt for a piece of writing. Just a paragraph, but try to make this paragraph represent you and your oeuvre.

# 17th November

*"In every bit of honest writing in the world, there is a base theme. Try to understand men, if you understand each other you will be kind to each other. Knowing a man well never leads to hate and nearly always leads to love."*
John Steinbeck

Today you're going to write a moral tale. A fable. First, pick the moral you want your story to impart. What life lesson do you have for us, oh wise writer? Have a gander at Aesop's *Fables* for some examples. The best ones have a simple moral. The dog and his reflection, for example:

A lucky dog has a big hunk of meat, but as he carries it across a bridge, he sees another dog with a big piece of meat in the water below (his reflection, of course). He opens his mouth to grab the other dog's meat, only to drop his own... and lose it in the water. D'oh! And the moral of the story is: don't be greedy, dog!

Either pick a moral from this list or think of your own:

- Don't underestimate yourself.

- Don't be selfish.

- Lead by example.

- Don't be quick to judge.

- No act of kindness is ever wasted.

Now pick some characters. Classically they are animal stories but write what you like (and if you do pick animals, think of some outside the usual range of Aesopian characters – no hares or tortoises, please). How about a camel, hippopotamus, jaguar, tree frog, skunk, ant, giant snail, badger, pigeon, bald eagle, raven, mini-pig, chihuahua, lobster, kangaroo, duck-billed platypus? When you've picked your moral and your characters, create your tale.

NOVEMBER

373

# 18th November

*"A word after a word after a word is power."*
Margaret Atwood

Happy birthday, **Margaret Atwood**! Atwood isn't only a master storyteller, but an exceptional writing teacher. Here's one of her best tips:

> *'Don't sit down in the middle of the woods. If you're lost in the plot or blocked, retrace your steps to where you went wrong. Then take the other road. And/or change the person. Change the tense. Change the opening page.'*

She's right. We mustn't allow ourselves to get stuck and then stop writing – it's too tempting to put down your work if you come to a difficult bit and then, you know… *accidentally* forget about it, and never pick it up again. Then it lurks like some unsavoury smell in your office; you know it's there, but you're too scared to open the drawer. So instead, pull it out, wrestle with it, face it and pummel it into submission.

Today, let's practise 'taking the other road'. Write a simple paragraph that describes a person going on a journey through a wood. And in the wood something happens.

Now, go back to the beginning and write it again in a different tense. Is it better?

Next, write it again but change the event. Go for something polar opposite. Red Riding Hood no longer meets a woodcutter in a forest, she meets a refugee. Or a very lost Amazon delivery driver.

Now, write it again but change your protagonist. Be radical. This is a game – the more fun you have, the better.

When you're done, consider which of your stories you liked the most? Which worked? Why? I'll bet you it wasn't the first one…

NOVEMBER

374

# 19th November

*"Song-writing is a very mysterious process.
It feels like creating something from nothing.
It's something I don't feel like I really control."*
Tracy Chapman

Many of Tracy Chapman's best songs feature characters that she's imagined. She is a lyricist and a storyteller. Today, let's take the first verse of her beautiful song 'Fast Car' and create a piece of writing telling the story of this encounter. Look the song lyrics up *and* listen to the song.

Ignore the later verses that give us more information about the speaker; in this exercise you are *solely* using the first verse as a jumping-off point. Ask yourself: who is speaking? Who owns the fast car? If they do own it. Maybe they borrowed it. Or stole it. Why is our speaker so desperate to get away? Any place is better than where? Why? What is the something they might make?

# 20th November

*"Isn't it nice to think that tomorrow is a new day
with no mistakes in it yet?"*
L. M. Montgomery

Today it's **Universal Children's Day**. So we are going to return to that old-school favourite, the A to Z, and use that as the backbone of our piece of writing. You're going to tell a story where each new sentence begins with the next letter of the alphabet. A twenty-six-line story. Don't overthink anything or plan what you're going to write about in advance – just start and see what happens!

NOVEMBER

# 21st November

"Reading is the finest teacher of how to write."
Annie Proulx

Today's exercise is about lounging in the joy of other people's words. As Annie Proulx wisely says, reading can be the very best teacher. Looking at how others choose to use words, whether it's to create character, atmosphere, a sense of poetry or to hook us in, today we're going to look to the experts and enjoy their delicious offerings.

Grab a pile of novels from your shelf (include some of your favourites). Sit down, make a big mug of something tasty and read the first paragraph of each story. Twice.

Read firstly for pleasure, then re-read, this time noting what the writer is doing. These first paragraphs will no doubt have been rewritten ad infinitum, as every writer knows that it's their principal opportunity to draw you in to the adventure – and if they don't hit the mark, they're out.

Some brilliant openings are so simple, in choice of words and sentiment:

Albert Camus' *The Stranger*: 'Mother died today.'

Or Ralph Ellison's *Invisible Man*: 'I am an invisible man.'

Others do quite the opposite, and yet have equal power, often because they are written in a distinctive narrative voice, in the first person. For example, the hero in Salinger's *The Catcher in the Rye* immediately accuses the reader of wanting to know the details of his upbringing, declaring, '*I don't feel like going into it, if you want to know the truth.*' This narrator is going to be tough, opinionated and uninterested in pandering to us. We know him – and like him – immediately.

A first line can deliver a shock, throwing us right in the story with no warning. Toni Morrison in *Paradise* does this so effectively it nearly knocks you over, whilst also setting her theme and world out front and centre: '*They shot the white girl first.*'

Other writers enjoy beginning with a trick, in order to hook our attention. Such as George Orwell's *1984*: '*It was a bright cold day in April and the clocks are striking thirteen.*'

Others use it to set the tone of the book you're about to enjoy. Perhaps most famously the delicious irony and wit that characterises Jane Austen's brilliant *Pride and Prejudice* is there is the very first line: '*It is a truth universally acknowledged, that a single man in possession of a good fortune, must be in want of a wife.*'

And others lounge around, scooping up words and throwing them at us to create a picture. Done well, this can be so rich and evocative that it can lift you out of your reading seat and plonk you straight into another world. Dylan Thomas does this exquisitely, using language in such a muscular, song-like way that you want to read it out loud. Take *Under Milk Wood*:

> '*To begin at the beginning: It is Spring, moonless night in the small town, starless and bible-black, the cobble streets silent and the hunched, courters'-and- rabbits' wood limping invisible down to the sloeblack, slow, black, crowblack, fishingboat-bobbing sea.*'

Which do you like? Do any of these examples have a style you think perhaps you might draw on? How do they use sentence length? Vocabulary? Punctuation? Mystery? How quickly do they jump in? Often faster than you might expect, knowing well that the quicker we're in, the more likely we are to stay. Which of these techniques might you employ in your writing?

# 22nd November

*"Life seems to go on without effort
when I am filled with music."*
George Eliot

So there's a cool button on the online encyclopaedia Wikipedia, which is 'Random article'. Head to Wikipedia and locate it in the dropdown menu on the left. Press it once and guess what: up comes a completely random article about... *something*!

Today's exercise is to write a narrative inspired by the topic of the random article. You're allowed three hits, just in case the first one is an absolute dud. But make sure you pick one of those three – the whole point is you get what you're given, and that anything can inspire a story. My first three were Honjō Castle in Japan; Jorge Alberto Lara Rivera, a Mexican lawyer; and the *Apotactis drimylota*, a species of moth from Mozambique.

If you don't have access to Wikipedia right now, then use my Mozambique moth as your chosen topic. They are in the family *Gelechiidae*, and were first discovered by Edward Meyrick in 1918. The wingspan is 14 to 16 mm. The forewings are grey, speckled with white, with a few black scales and small elongate blackish spots on the costa. So there you go. Who knew?

# 23rd November

Today, write a simple story on a piece of paper. Write in the third person, and chronologically. Write each new sentence on a new line. The story should have a very simple beginning, middle and ending, and fit on a single page.

Now, take a pair of scissors and cut the story up, each line being on a separate slip of paper.

Reorder it by throwing the pieces up in the air and choosing them randomly. How does it play out? Is it more interesting?

And then try reordering it strategically.

Which is the best piece of writing? Which most interesting? And how might you keep hold of this greater sense of playfulness and spontaneity in your work?

# 24th November

*"A well-composed book is a magic carpet on which we are wafted to a world that we cannot enter in any other way."*
Caroline Gordon

**Frances Hodgson Burnett**, whose birthday is today, wrote the beloved children's novel *The Secret Garden*. Today's task is to write a short story with that title – nothing to do with Burnett's story, but a new tale about a different 'secret garden'. Whose garden is it? Why is it secret? And who wants to uncover the secret?

I would strongly suggest getting outside for a walk to inspire you, and if it's not too cold, take your notebook and write outside. Try to capture something of the outside world – its sounds, smells, colours – in your writing today.

# 25th November

*"I'm not afraid of the darkness outside.
It's the darkness inside houses I don't like."*
Shelagh Delaney, *A Taste of Honey*

Choose a character from an existing story. Now pick a room in your house and go and sit in it. Now write about the room from the perspective of your character. Are they comfortable in it? Do they like it? What do they notice? What would their attitude towards it be? Might they be rude, intrigued, disgusted, enraptured?

A character's attitude to something we know well can tell us so much about them. Imagine the difference between a Royal's attitude to your messy little kitchen, compared to Paddington Bear – who might be fascinated by everything he sees and cause absolute havoc trying to find the marmalade.

# 26th November

*"'And what is the use of a book,' thought Alice,*
*'without pictures or conversation?'"*
Lewis Carroll, *Alice's Adventures in Wonderland*

Today, choose a story you like that you've written on an earlier day's exercise. Your task today is to illustrate it. Drawing can be a great way to spend time thinking about a story in your periphery, without worrying about getting words down. By drawing the story you are entering from a different perspective. What is interesting in your illustration which you hadn't realised or explored when you wrote it? I hope drawing it reinvigorates your interest in it – and perhaps even gives you inspiration to carry on.

# 27th November

*"In the end, the best stories are usually about a battle of good over evil – that has never changed."*
Cat Stevens

Make a list of characters we conventionally see as 'good' or 'evil.' Fairytale characters, historical characters, anyone who falls firmly into one of those camps. Then pick one favourite from each list – and swap elements of their personalities and narratives. So if you picked Snow White and Stalin, you now have a young girl lost in the woods with the ambition to become a great dictator, and a dictator with the innocence of a youthful girl who perhaps can talk to animals and likes wearing dresses.

You have the choice whether to write a story featuring both of these characters, or pick your favourite to be your protagonist. See what happens!

NOVEMBER

384

# 28th November

Today you're going to write a passage in Shakespeare's favourite rhythmic form: iambic pentameter. There are ten syllables in each line, in five (i.e *pent-*ameter) pairs of two syllables (iambs), each with a rhythm of 'weak-STRONG'. It sounds like a heartbeat: 'Di DUM di DUM di DUM di DUM di DUM'…

If LOVE be BLIND it BEST agrEES with NIGHT. (Juliet)

Once MORE unTO the BREACH, dear FRIENDS, once MORE. (Henry V)

I THINK that I would LIKE a CUP of TEA. (Me)

Have a go, it's fun!

# 29th November

*"Good books, like good friends, are few and chosen;
the more select, the more enjoyable."*
Louisa May Alcott

Today, on **Louisa May Alcott's birthday,** you are going to write a story using an element of her writing, in an unexpected way. The best known characters in *Little Women* are the four March sisters, Meg, Beth, Jo and Amy. But we're skirting them, and instead looking elsewhere for our inspiration. The book is peopled with other interesting characters, who never made it into popular culture in the same way. Time to raise them up from the dead!

For today's exercise, you are going to write a story using characters with the following names – all peripheral characters in *Little Women*. Feel free to use their personalities (if you know the book), or just use their names as a blank canvas to invent new personas. Choose at least four of the following as the cast for your story, work out who they are and see what happens:

- Marmee

- Dr Bangs

- Grace Vaughn

- The Hummels

- Demi

- Mrs Gardiner

- Laurie Lawrence (Alcott evidently ran out of ideas here)

386

# 30th November

**Mark Twain,** born on this day, was a great advocate of simple writing. Don't overwrite, he would say! Don't use too many adjectives. Every word should have a purpose... if you're going to use description, then make sure you *need* it to propel the story forward. The polar opposite of a writer like George Bernard Shaw, who joyfully slathers verbose description into his prose like whipped cream on a banana split. Who would win in a fight, Twain or Shaw? I'd like to see that. Let's put them into the ring, shall we?

For today's task, you're going to practise editing by giving Shaw the Twain treatment. The following passage is the opening to Shaw's novel *Love Among the Artists* (1900). Rewrite it, editing it with a Twainian sensibility. Choose what to keep, what to lose, which descriptions add something, which don't. And if you like, contemporise it, swap in words you prefer, change it as much as you like. Make it your own. And make sure you include at least one 'damn' – it is an excellent word and, I would argue, ought to be included in every good novel.

> *'One fine afternoon during the Easter holidays, Kensington Gardens were in their freshest Spring green and the steps of the Albert Memorial dotted with country visitors, who alternately conned their guide books and stared up at the golden gentleman under the shrine, trying to reconcile the reality with the description, whilst their Cockney friends, indifferent to shrine and statue, gazed idly at the fashionable drive below. One group in particular was composed of an old gentleman, intent upon the Memorial, a young lady intent upon her guide-book, and a young gentleman intent upon the young lady. She looked a woman of force and intelligence; and her boldly*

curved nose and chin, elastic step, upright carriage, resolute bearing, and thick black hair, secured at the base of the neck by a broad crimson ribbon, made those whom her appearance pleased think her strikingly handsome. The rest thought her strikingly ugly; but she would perhaps have forgiven them for the sake of the implied admission that she was at least not commonplace; for her costume, consisting of an ample black cloak lined with white fur, and a broad hat with red feather and underbrim of sea green silk, was of the sort affected by women who strenuously cultivate themselves, and insist upon their individuality. She was not at all like her father, the grey-haired gentleman who, scanning the Memorial with eager watery eyes, was uttering occasional ejaculations of wonder at the sum it must have cost. The young man, who might have been thirty or thereabout, was slight and of moderate structure. His fine hair, of a pale golden colour, already turning to a silvery brown, curled delicately over his temples, where it was beginning to wear away. A short beard set off his features, which were those of a man of exceptional sensitiveness and refinement. He was the Londoner of the part; and he waited with devoted patience whilst his companions satisfied their curiosity. It was pleasant to watch them, for he was not gloating over her, not she too conscious that she was making the sunshine brighter for him; and yet they were quite evidently young lovers, and as happy as people at their age know how to be.'

# December

# 1st December

Today is a simple writing-prompt day – and your prompt is:

*The cold.*

Write a poem, a scene or a story with this as the title. Take it in any way you want. And then have a nice cuppa to warm you up.

DECEMBER

391

# 2nd December

*"Creativity is just connecting things.*
*When you ask creative people how they did something,*
*they feel a little guilty because they didn't really do it,*
*they just saw something. It seemed obvious to them after*
*a while. That's because they were able to connect experiences*
*they've had and synthesize new things."*
Steve Jobs

Here's some things to connect. Your challenge today is to write a piece of prose involving the following six elements. Time to get creative!

- A character with an allergy.

- A small box.

- The line 'You said you weren't going to be here.'

- A rare moth.

- A metaphor of your choice.

- A strong smell.

# 3rd December

Some of the world's most popular books tap into the teenage experience of angst and frustration that stems from feeling misunderstood. Parents, get lost. Me and my friend know best. We are the one and only generation – and old people don't get it. Today you're going to write a piece in the voice of a teenager, at this tricky juncture in their lives. For inspiration, listen to The Who's fabulous song 'My Generation' – released on this day in 1965 – which is a full-bodied celebration of why it's cool to be young, and why older people suck. Which decade is your teenager living in? Be specific in your cultural references and in deciding what they are rebelling against – and try to write in this voice, keeping the tone of the speaker as your narrator.

And if you want further inspiration for a teenage voice as narrator, check out *The Catcher in the Rye*.

# 4th December

*"A thousand words will not leave so deep an impression as one deed."*
Henrik Ibsen

Ibsen's seminal play *A Doll's House* was published on this day in 1879. In the play, Nora is trapped by her circumstances... hence the title. A wife in a bourgeois landscape, she finds herself drowning in expectations, the pressure to be a good mother and a good wife. She realises that her only chance of true happiness is to run away, leaving her children and her husband, a deeply problematic and culturally unacceptable decision.

Such an act would have caused an outrage. It arguably still would – but in the late-nineteenth century it was unheard of. Yet Ibsen tells Nora's story with such empathy... to the extent that he was forced to write an alternative ending in which she (more acceptably) decides to put her family first and stay, at the expense of her own happiness.

The play's radical, empathetic tone renders it one of the most explosive and enduring plays ever to be staged. Many, me included, would argue it is as relevant today as it was at the time.

Your task today is to write a scene or narrative of the same title, *A Doll's House*, about a character trapped by their circumstances. It could be on any theme in which the protagonist is limited by their identity, be it gender, race, age, sexuality; something that makes them unusual, an outsider, a pariah. Put their emotional drama at the heart of your story. Give them a dilemma. The heart of your drama is the investigation of their choice. Do they submit and become what the others want them to be, or do they break the mould and follow their heart?

# 5th December

*"I write entirely to find out what I'm thinking, what I'm looking at, what I see and what it means. What I want and what I fear... We tell ourselves stories in order to live."*

Joan Didion

**Joan Didion**'s most famous book, *A Year of Magical Thinking*, is a moving account of the year after her husband died, during which she grapples with, and tries to make sense of her grief. It's a hugely popular book with people who are experiencing loss, as she writes so candidly about the experience, challenges and hope that can spring from remembering a loved one.

In a nod to the book, and in honour of her birthday today, your task is to choose someone you have lost. Anyone who impacted your life in some way. Or, if you don't know anyone (lucky you), then choose something that has ended: a time in your life, a place you left, a band you once loved.

Think of a memory of them. Write down everything you remember. How does it make you feel? How did they inspire you? How did they impact you at the time, and how since? What is different, reflecting back now? Imagine if you knew you'd be looking back on this after they'd gone – how does that shift your perspective? Make this into a short piece of life writing: an autobiographical piece in your own voice. This act of writing will help you to remember, in addition to allowing you to write in your most authentic voice. It's another way this person has inspired you.

# 6th December

*"Learn the rules like a pro,*
*so you can break them like an artist."*
Pablo Picasso

Today you're going to break some writing rules. Choose one of the following much touted 'essential tips' (some of which, ahem, I may have encouraged at various points in these pages) and write a piece today that flagrantly disregards that rule. Be a rebel. Go on. I dare you. Here are the rules you can choose to flout:

- *Write what you know.*

Today write about something you know nothing about. I mean – let's be honest – it's going to be a better piece of writing if you put a few minutes into researching this thing, but hey, break the rules, do what you want! Write with an utter disregard for fact and experience – let your imagination do the work.

- *Write with focus; less is more; don't digress.*

Sometimes diversions are excellent – and very diverting. Maybe they're more interesting than your plot. In Dave Eggers' *A Heartbreaking Work of Staggering Genius,* he constructs much of the text as footnotes – then writes footnotes to the footnotes, meaning a good chunk of the book is entirely digressions. And he is a staggering genius. So take a leaf out of his book and 'sidebar', as they say in the States.

- *Write a likeable protagonist.*

A good protagonist must be someone we can empathise with, even if they're troubled, right? They should have enough heart – and you must, as a writer, construct them with such authenticity that we still see and understand their bad deeds. Nope. Not today. Today go for gold and make your protagonist an absolute, irredeemable bastard. Sock it to us. We can take it.

DECEMBER

# 7th December

*"Make up a story... For our sake and yours, forget your name in the street; tell us what the world has been to you in the dark places and in the light. Don't tell us what to believe, what to fear. Show us belief's wide skirt and the stitch that unravels fear's caul."*

Toni Morrison
(from her Nobel Lecture on this day in 1993)

Today, your task is to go out for a walk. While you are working, see if you can spot:

- A person you find intriguing.

- An interesting location for a story.

- An object that surprises you.

Mull on these as you walk. Then, when you return, write a short piece with these as the three ingredients: protagonist, location and a story-starting object.

# 8th December

*"I can survive well enough on my own,
if given the proper reading material."*
Sarah J. Maas

Today's simple task is to write a list of all the ideas you have for future stories. Set a timer for ten minutes and scribble down everything you might like to write about when you have the time (note to you: you *do* have the time; you just need to cordon it off, then sit on your ass and do it).

When you're done, rewrite the list in priority order as a list of stories 'to do'. Maybe decorate it so it looks zingy and will catch your eye. Now put the list somewhere you can see it. There's your inspiration right there…

DECEMBER

# 9th December

…Today you're going to pick one of the stories from yesterday's list and write that!

Up to you whether you draw it first as a comic-strip-style beat sheet to help you think it through visually.

# 10th December

*"If I can stop one heart from breaking,
I shall not live in vain."*
Emily Dickinson

**Emily Dickinson,** born on this day, was a rebellious and brilliant poet. She challenged the very form of poetry by writing in unconventional ways, chopping up her paper into shapes to reflect the themes of her poetry, and writing with other materials – on the back of envelopes, objects, all sorts.

Today, pick a different material from usual. You're going to write on something that gives character to your work. What might it be? And who might write on it? Is it the back of a bill? Or a cocktail napkin? Or a bar mat? A leaf? A piece of bark? A scrap of cardboard? Or an aeroplane sick bag (depending, of course, on where you are and what access you have to materials).

Write as a character who is compelled to write on this specific object because of who they are and their circumstances. Write as them, and use the shape and size of the material to dictate what you write.

# 11th December

*"What are men to rocks and mountains?"*
Jane Austen, *Pride and Prejudice*

Mountains, nature, epic landscapes, inspiring vistas – it's **International Mountains Day**! Today your task is to find a painting of a landscape you find inspiring and write an opening paragraph to a novel set in this place. Remember, it doesn't have to be beautiful.

Perhaps you are inspired by a painting of a chicken factory, full of interesting characters and feathery drama. Perhaps it's a Bruegel painting or a medieval fresco depicting the weird creatures of Hell eating each other. Perhaps it's a simple view of the sea. Whichever you pick, you are only writing the *beginning* of a story. Use the specific details of what you see in the picture to build the world, tempt us in, encourage us to want to read on.

# 12th December

*"The English language is an arsenal of weapons.*
*If you are going to brandish them without checking to see*
*whether or not they are loaded, you must expect to have*
*them explode in your face from time to time."*
Stephen Fry

We love characterful, extraordinary, unusual words. Today, go to a dictionary and find five words you don't know. Pick good ones, you're on rations here. Write them down, with their definitions, then construct a passage or a poem that uses all of them.

# 13th December

*"Please, no matter how we advance technologically, please don't abandon the book. There is nothing in our material world more beautiful than the book."*
Patti Smith

Let's talk about midpoints. Conventionally, the midpoint is the turning point, in which the character realises the problem you set them up with at the beginning, and then makes a change, *thinking* they know how to solve it... but they don't! There's more drama to come – as usually the second half is characterised by everything going wrong. But that's for later; let's now look at the midpoint.

Often the trickiest moment in a story, it's the part of a conventional character arc in which your character has their vital turning point. The emotional pivot, their change from one direction to a new direction that propels them towards the end of the story.

If your character was desperate for love but had a crippling fear of intimacy, this is the moment they face that, act on it and determine to make a change to get together with the person of their dreams. If your character wants to save their children from disaster but has to get on a plane to do it – and they are desperately scared of flying... this is the moment they face their fear.

Your task today is to write three midpoint scenarios. Work out what the change is by choosing three characters, giving them each a problem, and working out what happens *now* that gives them the means and motivation to tackle it.

# 14th December

*"Use all your seasoning sparingly."*
Shirley Jackson

Perhaps **Shirley Jackson** didn't mean this literally, but let's take her advice for real on her birthday.

Go to the kitchen and pick a spice or condiment. Try it. Sniff it, taste it, consider its quality. This spice is going to be at the heart of your story today. It is the essence on which the action turns. Where does it take you? Is it za'atar from a market in Marrakesh? Is it moutarde from the balmy South of France? Is it malt vinegar from a chippy in Harrogate?

Your choice must feature in your story, but also try to use the flavour of it to give your descriptive sensory world a tone that matches the taste. Think about the colours you draw from this spice too to give your story depth and compelling detail.

# 15th December

*"You can never get a cup of tea large enough
or a book long enough to suit me."*
C. S. Lewis

Tea is a great comfort, isn't it? A lovely, warming, soulful, calming delight. Your task today is to make a cup of your favourite flavour, pour yourself a brew then find a comfy chair, set your timer for ten minutes, and sit and daydream while you drink. See what bubbles up, and at the end, scribble it down.

If you find your mind wandering to what you ought to put on your shopping list, have a little word with yourself and another sip, and get back to your more magical thinking. This is meditative tea-drinking, not life-planning time. If you have thoughts that aren't helpful, just see them, dismiss them and move straight on.

Thinking time that is free from distractions is an invaluable resource for a writer. Taking time to allow your mind to wander is often when the good ideas rise up.

DECEMBER

# 16th December

*"Science-fiction writers, I am sorry to say,*
*really do not know anything. We can't talk about science,*
*because our knowledge of it is limited and unofficial,*
*and usually our fiction is dreadful."*
Philip K. Dick

On **Philip K. Dick's birthday,** here's a writing prompt for you today. Science fiction, here we come.

Your story begins with a normal family on a normal day in a normal town, who wake up to find a crack in the earth in their garden. Yes, these town-dwellers are lucky enough to have a garden – this is fiction, after all.

Standing at the edge of the crack, a strange rumble begins. They peer in. As they do, the crack begins to widen. What they see down there, you would scarcely believe…

What is it? And what happens next?

Go!

# 17th December

*"Writing is its own reward."*
Henry Miller

Sometimes good writing is just about seeing from a different perspective. Today, find a place in your house with some wall space. Lie on your back with your feet up against the wall, shuffle your bum up to the wall behind to get snug, and take a view of the ceiling.

Two things will happen. Firstly, the blood will begin to drain from your legs back towards your heart and head thereby – supposedly – energising you. (On any normal day, if you feel tired and in need of a bit of pep, try lying in this position. It really works, I promise.)

Secondly, you will see the room from a position you're most probably not used to. Spend a few minutes staring at the ceiling. Imagine if everything was the other way up and you lived on the ceiling. Who might you be? How might life on the ceiling play out, in this upside-down landscape.

Today's task is to write a story set upside down.

DECEMBER

# 18th December

*"No matter what people tell you,
words and ideas can change the world."*
Tom Schulman, *Dead Poets Society*

If you want to be a storyteller for a living – whether it's a novelist, playwright, film-maker, poet – you have to be good at pitching your ideas. It's a vital skill: to summarise your proposal in bite-sized, tempting morsels to encourage a producer/publisher/audience to gobble the whole thing up. But the task often flummoxes writers, who can't quite believe that a publisher doesn't want to cold-read your entire eight-hundred-page epic, and instead they insist on just the opening and – you've guessed it – a summary.

So, in order to practise (and to save you right now writing the said eight-hundred-page epic), choose a novel or film you know and love, and write the back-cover text for it. In a couple of paragraphs try to set the scene, set up the action and draw the reader into the story. What choice details might compel someone to pick this tale? And what hook can you dangle to entice them to read on? When you've done one, pick a second novel – one with a contrasting tone – and write the blurb for that book. It's a great way to practise pitching a story; a skill you'll undoubtedly need as your career, should you want it, goes flying!

# 19th December

*"Yet, I had nothing else to tell; unless, indeed,
I were to confess (which might be of less moment still),
that no one can ever believe this Narrative, in the reading,
more than I believed it in the writing."*
Charles Dickens, *David Copperfield*

Today you're going to write a celebration song. It can commemorate anything you like. Perhaps it's ***A Christmas Carol***, which was published on this day in 1843, perhaps it's an ode to cheese, perhaps it's a rap about puppies, perhaps it's a testimony about your dad's love of bendable plastic. Whatever your tipple, write a song in praise of something great. If you're entirely unmusical, take the shape and melody of a song you know well and write new words for it. Who knows, it might be the next Christmas number one...

DECEMBER

# 20th December

*"While drawing I discover what I really want to say."*
Dario Fo

Today, gather a pencil and a piece of paper. Put some music on if you like. Set a timer for twenty minutes. Draw a scene.

It can take place anywhere, at any time. Start by drawing two people. What are they doing? Who are they? What's going on? Put some objects in it. Build their world. Add more people.

Draw some action happening. What's going down? What is the drama? Draw people's reactions. Is it a joyous event? Or a tragedy? Or a world-changing moment? Be inventive – this is your imagination – *anything* can happen!

Carry on adding detail, building the scenario in your mind. Stop when the timer goes and write the scene. It doesn't have to be a whole story – it's this key scene in isolation – perhaps you leave us on a cliffhanger. Leave us with a sense of excitement about what happens next.

And remember next time you are scrabbling around for an idea that you can start with just a small section of a scenario – just two people – and build from there.

# 21st December

*"It's not what you look at that matters, but what you see."*
Henry David Thoreau

Today you're going to source your own inspiration for a story. Take a paper bag or a shopping bag… I like the rudimentary retro idea of a brown paper bag, because I'm an old romantic. You might be more of a designer-tote type, or a Tesco plastic kinda guy.

Whatever, leave the house and go for a walk. Potter around, and as you do, you're going to collect four objects. Perhaps they're items from nature – a twig, a skeleton leaf, a stone – perhaps something dropped or abandoned – a pen lid, a salt sachet. Or something.

Put the four objects in your paper bag and head home. Take them out, inspect each one, and, setting a timer for two minutes for each object, write down every thought that comes to mind when you look at it. Some concrete facts: What does it look and feel like? Other ideas can be more abstract and require creative thinking: What's the object's backstory? Who did it belong to? What does it represent?

Take a look at all four objects and your lists of facts and ideas about each one, and then combine whichever ideas excite you most to write a short piece.

Note: If you're working through this book in chronological order, read tomorrow's entry today – as you need to set an alarm!

411

# 22nd December

*"There is something really magic about the couple of hours before dawn. You're recharged, the day before is gone, but there are no requirements. You don't belong to anybody, to anything. That time lends itself to lyricism because of the repetitive nature of insomniac thoughts."*
Kae Tempest

Hopefully by the time you read this, it's not too late for this exercise. But if it is, swap them around; do tomorrow's exercise today, and get up early tomorrow to do this exercise instead.

Today, you are going to set an alarm for forty-five minutes before you usually get up, so you can appreciate the magic that **Kae Tempest** describes at dawn. (Today's their birthday.)

When the alarm goes off and it's dark and you don't want to get out of bed, remember this is your MAGIC TIME! The time before everyone else is up and needing stuff, crashing about and intruding on your bandwidth. Now is secret time, *your* time. Quick, embrace it!

Get up out of bed, splash your face with water, grab a coffee and sit to write. You are going to set a timer for fifteen minutes and free-write. That means just start writing. Don't filter, don't edit, write whatever spills out, unprompted. Try to keep on writing without stopping.

Something will bubble up. Something always does. And this special time, this borrowed magical morning time is a way you can access that slightly subconscious, half-awake dream state, and *still* have time to work on it later, if your mental fishing net catches a whopper.

I love this time in the morning. You can train yourself to embrace it too.

# 23rd December

*"The moment of inspiration can come from memory, or language, or the imagination, or experience – anything that makes an impression forcibly enough for language to form."*
Carol Ann Duffy

Today, let's think about colour. Have a look online at the colour wheel. It gives you a palette, and shows you which colours are complementary (those opposite each other) or analogous (adjacent colours).

Today's exercise is to pick four colours from the colour wheel and to use each to create a character. How does each colour make you feel? Who does it evoke for you? You don't need to think too literally – we're not necessarily talking people who wear these colours. Think instead of the feeling that each colour gives you, and how that might relate to a personality.

When you have constructed four characters, stick them in a room together and write the dialogue scene. Who teams up with who? Do sparks fly between complementary colours? Is there a clash of tones and personalities? Colour can also be a handy tool in helping to develop characters. It's also a short cut to ensuring variety in the people you are writing. In any writing project, ask yourself what shade your characters are to you, and see if this might help colour them in a bit.

# 24th December

*"Any word you have to hunt for in a thesaurus is the wrong word. There are no exceptions to this rule."*
Stephen King

Today, let's do something fun. Your task is to find something delicious to eat, which – if you're celebrating Christmas tomorrow – will hopefully be easy. Choose an absolute treat. Now think of a character who – for a particular reason – would love this delicacy more than anything else in the world. Who would *most* enjoy this experience right now? What would make this moment extraordinary? Think of your own enjoyment, then imagine that in technicolour.

- Is it the astronaut who has only eaten dried foods for the past three years now about to eat a yogurt?

- Is it the athlete returning from a desert marathon to have a cold, sweet ice-lolly?

- Is it the kid who's never been allowed ice cream and is, for the first time, allowed to eat a *whole tub*?!

Fill your boots – eat it all in the name of character research! Eat slowly, savouring it, taking in the detailed sensorial experience on all five senses and the emotional pleasure you experience. Notice if it's cool, smooth, spicy, piquant, oleaginous? Then write a passage describing that character's experience.

I hope you choose something delicious.

DECEMBER

414

# 25th December

*"I will honour Christmas in my heart, and try to keep it all the year. I will live in the Past, the Present, and the Future. The Spirits of all Three shall strive within me. I will not shut out the lessons that they teach."*
Charles Dickens, *A Christmas Carol*

**Merry Christmas!** Or **Happy Holidays**, whichever you celebrate. Your task today is to rest, eat, drink and be thoroughly merry. Hug all your family, drink all the wine, celebrate till you drop, full as an egg, into a heap on the sofa.

If you really want a writing task, here's a little word game I used to play with my grandma at Christmas. You can play it on your own or with one of your drunken relatives. It's called the Christmas Cat.

Think of a word with 'cat' in it. Now, draw a picture of a cat representing that word. Perhaps you draw a long, wriggly bug with a cat's face (CATerpillar). Or a bunch of cats making a racket by meowing through the night (CATerwaul). Or a cat trimming a hedge with big scissors (seCATeurs). If you're playing with a group, take turns guessing what each other has drawn. If you're playing solo, just see how many you can do, and give yourself a big pat on the back. Then finish that tub of Quality Street.

# 26th December

*"Forget the books you want to write.
Think only of the book you are writing"*
Henry Miller

If you're celebrating Christmas, today is **Boxing Day**, otherwise known as 'Walk Off Christmas Lunch' Day, 'Escape from Relatives' Day or 'Watch a Christmas Movie' Day.

Your task is to write a plot for a proper Christmas film. There's plenty of genres to choose from, from the classics (*It's a Wonderful Life*, *Scrooge*, *The Muppet Christmas Carol*) to the adventures set at Christmas (*Home Alone*, *Die Hard*), the fantasies (*The Polar Express*, *Elf*, *The Santa Clause*) and the romcoms (*The Holiday*, *Love Actually*, *Sleepless in Seattle*).

Choose your genre and write a movie pitch for the next Christmas classic. And if you're feeling like you've had quite enough of Christmas by now, or don't celebrate it at all, write an *anti*-Christmas story, about a bad Christmas: Grinch-like, disastrous, the end of festive cheer.

And, of course, feel free to substitute Christmas with a festivity or celebration of your choice. Make sure your movie has a strong opening, a dramatic problem that needs solving, a turn around the midpoint, and a fully festive jingly ending.

# 27th December

*"Nothing is really work unless you would rather be doing something else."*
J. M. Barrie

J. M. Barrie's much-loved classic **Peter Pan** was first performed on stage on this day in 1904. It is essentially about a boy looking for a family, and today we're going to dive into that theme. Your task is to find a photo in a family album. Pick a photo with several people in it – a group shot at a wedding is ideal, or a picture of a picnic or barbecue at the beach. The older the photograph – and the less well you know the people in it – the better.

Now, rather than writing about the people who stand out at the centre of the picture, look for the outliers. Who is caught in the background? Who is the reluctant relative at the back of the shot? Write a short piece as them, set in this moment. What's going on with them? Why are they here? What's the story we *don't* know behind this picture… the bit, if you didn't look closely, you would have missed? Often the underdogs and the outliers make the most interesting protagonists.

# 28th December

*"The pleasure of reading a story and wondering what will come next for the hero is a pleasure that has lasted for centuries and, I think, will always be with us."*
Stan Lee

Today, just for fun, we're going to do really short stories. And when I say 'really short', I mean *really* short.

- Set your timer for four minutes. Write a short story, with the first line 'It was the last thing I expected when I walked into the...' Go!

- Write until the timer beeps and stop. The aim, if you possibly can, is to finish the story in that time.

- Now, set your timer for three minutes. This time your first line is 'As the stuffing came tumbling out, something glinted.' Go!

- Now, set your timer for two minutes. Your first line is going to be 'He scratched and scratched...' Go!

- Now, set your timer for one minute. Yikes! Your first line is going to be 'Newt popped his head out above the gate.'

- Now set your timer for thirty seconds. Your first word is going to be 'Bang!'

Phew! Sets your adrenalin going, doesn't it? Did you get better at writing quickly and just trusting the first thing that came into your head? You have no time to think when you're writing that quickly. And sometimes – just sometimes – that can be a very good thing.

# 29th December

"I have never started a poem yet whose end I knew.
Writing a poem is discovering."
Robert Frost

Time to write a poem without knowing what's going to happen. Let whatever tumbles out, tumble out.

Write your poem with the following words at the beginning of each new line:

I…
Have…
No…
Idea…

Where…
This…
Will…
Go…

Surprise…
Is…
Always…
Best…

# 30th December

*"Poetry is a solitary process. One does not write poetry for the masses. Poetry is a self-involved, lofty pursuit. Songs are for the people. When I'm writing a song, I imagine performing it. I imagine giving it. It's a different aspect of communication. It's for the people."*
Patti Smith

**Patti Smith,** born today, writes the most remarkable lyrics. She is a true storyteller. Have a look at her songs, and marvel at the breadth and invention of the stories she tells.

Today's task is to write a character monologue or a short piece inspired by a verse of Patti's lyrics. If you don't know her music, have a browse. It's rich pickings for both story and character. One of her great virtues is her ability to use simple yet potent language. She often uses monosyllables, Anglo-Saxon words (black, hot, horse), but uses them in a context which pulls us in.

In the first verse of 'Kimberly', for example, she uses clean, monosyllabic words to paint a vivid picture for us: *'The wall is high, the barn black / The babe in my arms in her swaddling clothes'*, before then pulling the rug out from under us with her next line: *'And I know soon the sky will split'*.

It's unexpected, forceful, brilliant. All single syllables – all cut to the quick. This song, the first verse in particular, would be a good choice for your monologue inspiration, but there are plenty of others to choose from. Take your time to enjoy her work – it's magnificent.

# 31st December

*"Finishing a good book is like leaving a good friend."*
William Feather

Good lord, you did it! It's **New Year's Eve** – the end of the year – and you made it! Perhaps you have 'completed' this book, and studiously tackled all 365 different tasks and exercises (or 366 if it's a leap year)? Whether you have or not: congratulations, you completed another year! You did it! You're alive! And you are clearly thriving... anyone who has the capacity to think creatively as a daily practice must be.

Well done, you.

Thank you for sticking with me. Thank you for contributing the marvel that is imagination and creativity to the world. Even if it's in the tiniest way, even if not a single soul has or will ever read your work, it's made you a wee bit happier, or calmer, or excited about stories, that is a glorious thing.

Keep it up! Unless you started religiously on 1st January, and completed every day's task, there will be tasks in this book that you haven't done yet, so persevere. And if you've done every exercise – you promise – write to me and let me know – and I'll write another book. Or hell, write to me anyway, who doesn't love a letter in the post?

Your task today is in celebration of the end of the year – like the end of a wonderful book (or a dreadful one that you can throw down and think, 'Thank GOD I don't have to deal with that interminable tome any more'). Whether you had a great year or can't wait to see the back of it, it's now time for a new start.

What I'd love you to do today is to make a plan for what your *next* year of writing will look like. What do you want to write? What have you written this year that was exciting? Which ideas do you want to return to? Do you want to give a new genre a go? Are you finally going to write that novel? If so, give yourself a daily word count to hit – it's a great motivator. Are you planning to read a load of new books? If so, write that down as a resolution. Make a plan – and *do it*! But make your plans realistic. Better to have one simple achievable resolution than twenty that you'll never keep. Say you'll write one page a day, not four novels by Easter.

Now write your dream list: 'Next year I would love to...'

Make it as long as you like. Dream big. Then go off and live that dream.

It's been a pleasure spending time with you. Keep thinking creatively in the year ahead. It will exercise your brain, fuel your imagination and lift your heart. What better way to start a year. So keep going. You are wonderful.

# About the Author

Jessica Swale is an Olivier Award-winning playwright, screenwriter and director. She trained at the Royal Central School of Speech and Drama and the University of Exeter, but learnt most of what she knows messing around in rehearsal rooms.

Jessica works across film, TV and theatre, depending on the medium a story calls for, and how much of an adventure the work offers up. Since she realised that you get to live wherever your film is set, she's currently writing a bunch of films set on the Italian Riviera.

As a filmmaker, her work includes *Merv* (MGM/Amazon) starring Zooey Deschanel, Charlie Cox and Gus the dog; *Summerland* (as writer/director; Lionsgate); *Horrible Histories: The Movie* (Altitude) and *Call My Agent!* (Amazon/Bron). Her short film *Leading Lady Parts* (BBC) became a viral hit with over twenty million views, *most* of which were not her family. Current projects include *Nell Gwynn* and *Shrewd!* (both Working Title), a new series for Netflix and an original series for the BBC.

As a playwright, Jessica has written the book for *Paddington: The Musical* for Sonia Friedman Productions, working with songwriter Tom Fletcher and a furry brown bear. Her plays include *Nell Gwynn* (Shakespeare's Globe/West End), which won the Olivier Award for

Best New Comedy; *Blue Stockings*, now a set text on the GCSE Drama syllabus; *Thomas Tallis* (Sam Wanamaker Playhouse); *All's Will That Ends Will* (Bremer Shakespeare Company); adaptations of *The Jungle Book* (Northampton); *Far from the Madding Crowd*, *Sense and Sensibility* (Watermill Theatre); *The Secret Garden*, *Stig of the Dump* (Grosvenor Park); and radio play *Love* [*sic*] for BBC Radio 4.

Jessica set up Red Handed Theatre Company in 2005, for whom she directed *The Rivals* starring Celia Imrie, *The Busy Body*, *Someone Who'll Watch Over Me* and *The Belle's Stratagem*, which won her a nomination for Best Director at the Evening Standard Awards. She has directed for many theatres including The Park, Shakespeare's Globe, Salisbury Playhouse, The Watermill, and theatres in Canada and the USA. She is an Associate Artist with International NGO Youth Bridge Global, for whom she has directed Shakespeare productions in Bosnia and Herzegovina, Kosovo and the Marshall Islands, where she also learnt to spear-fish. It's not as useful a life skill as she hoped.

Jessica is the author of three books in Nick Hern Books' bestselling series of drama games – *Drama Games for Classrooms and Workshops*, *...for Devising*, and *...for Rehearsals* – and a study guide to her play *Blue Stockings* (written with Lois Jeary).

She lives in London – and sometimes New York – with her photographer husband and Newt, their overly affectionate Cocker Spaniel.

# Acknowledgements

This is a book about sources of inspiration… which makes writing acknowledgements very tricky, as I have been lucky enough to find many muses in my creative meanderings towards making this book.

The directors I have worked with, the writers, mentors and mentees, my fellow writing tutors at Arvon, my acting compadres, the artists I'm lucky to count amongst my best friends – all have dropped trails of inspirational bread crumbs which have led the way towards this book.

In terms of making an actual book out of those crumbs and baking it into this tasty loaf, special thanks go to Matt Applewhite and all at Nick Hern Books, to Helen Mumby and the team at The Soho Agency, to Frank Wuliger and the Gersh agency crew, to Laura Symons and the publicists at Premier, and to the brilliant Matilda Morrogh-Ryan. To the magicians of the imagination who so kindly read and commented on the proofs – Deborah, Emerald, Inua, Jack, Kate, Sabrina, Tom and Zooey – I know it's a great act of generosity to support someone else's creative endeavour when you're all buried knee-deep in your own – thank you all.

Fundamentally, I have to thank my mum, and her mum before her, who always encouraged us to find entire worlds with only pen and paper. And as I write this on my firefly-lit, Vin Santo-infused honeymoon in Umbria, to my other favourite muse, Michael: *grazie mille per tutto.*

\* \* \*

The author and publisher gratefully acknowledge the following quoted works:

*Love and Information* copyright © 2012 Caryl Churchill; reproduced by permission of Nick Hern Books Ltd. *American Dirt* copyright © 2020 Jeanine Cummins, published by Tinder Press, an imprint of Hachette UK; reproduced with permission of the licensor through PLSclear. *Howl and Other Poems* © 1956, 2010 Allen Ginsberg LLC, reproduced by permission of The Wylie Agency (UK) Limited. 'Jack Kerouac, The Art of Fiction No. 41' copyright © 1968 The Paris Review Foundation, Inc., reproduced by permission of The Wylie Agency (UK) Limited. '*One Perfect Rose*' in *The Collected Work of Dorothy Parker*, published by Penguin Random House USA. 'You're' in *Ariel* copyright © 1965 Sylvia Plath, published by Faber and Faber Ltd and reprinted with permission. *Cannery Row* copyright © 1945 John Steinbeck, published by Penguin Random House. *The Glass Menagerie* by Tennessee Williams, copyright © 1945, renewed 1973 by The University of the South; reproduced by permission of Georges Borchardt, Inc. for the University of the South; all rights reserved.

The publisher will be glad to rectify in any future editions any errors or omissions brought to its attention.

ACKNOWLEDGEMENTS

# Index of Quoted
# Writers, Artists and Thinkers

INDEXES

# Index of Exercises

431

INDEXES

1 December, 2 December,
6 December, 9 December,
17 December, 26 December

**Structure**   19 January, 20 January,
31 January, 19 February, 25 March,
29 May, 5 August, 2 September,
6 October, 7 October, 8 October,
13 December

**Timed Exercises**   30 January,
3 February, 22 February, 13 March,
14 March, 22 April, 27 April, 6 May,
18 May, 25 May, 1 June, 17 June,
23 June, 24 June, 30 June, 3 July,
10 July, 13 July, 18 July, 7 August,
8 August, 10 August, 15 August,

16 September, 21 October,
25 October, 29 October, 7 November,
8 December, 20 December,
22 December, 28 December

**Vocabulary**   7 January, 15 January,
18 January, 9 February, 15 February,
22 February, 1 March, 3 March,
8 March, 15 March, 20 March,
31 March, 4 April, 8 April, 13 April,
22 April, 25 May, 31 May, 1 June,
11 June, 30 June, 3 July, 26 July,
5 September, 13 September,
24 September, 16 October,
3 November, 5 November,
16 November, 12 December,
25 December

INDEXES

**www.nickhernbooks.co.uk**

@nickhernbooks